STUDENT-CENTERED TEACHING & LEARNING

Proceedings of the 2018 Pedagogicon

Edited by:
Russell Carpenter
Shirley O'Brien
Jennifer Fairchild
Randi Polk

NEW FORUMS PRESS INC.

Published in the United States of America
by New Forums Press, Inc.1018 S. Lewis St.
Stillwater, OK 74074
www.newforums.com

Copyright © 2019 by New Forums Press, Inc.

All rights reserved. No part of this publication may be reproduced or transmitted in any form or by any means, electronic or mechanical, including photocopy, or any information storage or retrieval system, without permission in writing from the publisher.

Library of Congress Cataloging-in-Publication Data Pending

This book may be ordered in bulk quantities at discount from New Forums Press, Inc., P.O. Box 876, Stillwater, OK 74076 [Federal I.D. No. 73 1123239]. Printed in the United States of America.

ISBN 10: 1-58107-333-X
ISBN 13: 978-1-58107-333-1

Cover design by Melissa Abney.

Table of Contents

Introduction to the 2018 Proceedings – Student-Centered Teaching and Learning v
    Randi Polk, Shirley O'Brien, Jennifer Fairchild, & Russell Carpenter,
    Eastern Kentucky University

Metacognition

Using Metacognitive Microactivities to Engage Students.. 1
    Wren Mills, Western Kentucky University

Critical Reading Skills of Graduate Occupational Therapy Students: A Scholarship
    of Teaching and Learning Project.. 5
    Leslie J. Hardman & MaryEllen Thompson, Eastern Kentucky University

Creative Writing as Queer Process Pedagogy in the Straight-Aligned
    Post-Secondary Composition Classroom 9
    James McClure, Eastern Kentucky University

Metacognition: Using Critical Reading Strategies to Promote Critical Thinking
    and Clinical Reasoning... 13
    Shirley Peganoff O'Brien & Camille Skubik-Peplaski, Eastern Kentucky University

Student Perception of Mindfulness Strategies' Impact on Student Learning 19
    Jennifer Hight, Eastern Kentucky University

New Technologies and Emerging Trends

Active Learning: Blending the Classroom in 3 Dimensions 25
    Thad Crews, Western Kentucky University

Podcasts for (Inter)active Teaching and Learning 31
    Jason P. Johnston, Diane N. Loeffler, & Blake L. Jones, University of Kentucky

Designing an Online Course that Promotes Deeper Learning... 37
    Firm Faith Watson, Murray State University

Jigsaw Virtual Field Trips: Blending Teaching Strategies to Leverage Online Resources................... 49
    April R. Hatcher & Sara B. Police, University of Kentucky

New Technologies and How to Use Them: 3D and Makerspaces Demystified 53
    Lesia Lennex & Justin Elswick, Morehead State University

Student Engagement

Adjusting Teaching Practices to Benefit Generation Z Learners... 59
    Gaby Bedetti, Eastern Kentucky University

Reinventing Student Engagement: The Role of In-class Simulation 71
   Keri New, Catherine Edwards, Shannon Shumaker, & Brooke Bentley,
   Eastern Kentucky University

Team-Based Learning: An Opportunity to Model Student-Centered Learning 77
in a Teacher Preparation Course
   Michelle A. Gremp, Eastern Kentucky University

Best Practices for Engaging Introverts 83
   Susan Weaver, Glenda Warren, & Chris Lockhart, University of the Cumberlands

Going Back in Time: Designing Student Learning through Oral History Interviews 87
   Melony A. Shemberger, Murray State University

Teachers as Students, Students as Teachers

First Steps in Qualitative Research 91
   Aimee M. Cloutier & Ella L. Ingram, Rose-Hulman Institute of Technology

Incorporating Soft Skills for Student Success 97
   Lynda N. Donathan & Anthony T. Dotson, Morehead State University

Engaging Agents: Students as Class Facilitators for Academic Articles 101
   Tanya Robertson, University of Louisville

Resistive Pedagogy: Student-Facilitated Learning and Literacy through Zines 105
   Jessica Vaught, Eastern Kentucky University

Using Assessment Data to Create Targeted Instructor Training 111
   John Strada, Krista M. Kimmel, & Jennifer L. Fairchild, Eastern Kentucky University

Introduction to the 2018 Proceedings – Student-Centered Teaching and Learning

Randi Polk, Shirley O'Brien, Jennifer Fairchild, & Russell Carpenter
Eastern Kentucky University

Introduction

In both research and practice, the role of teacher and learner has shifted over recent years. In the traditional approach to college teaching, the instructor was the "sage on the stage" and students passively received their messages. The dynamics of the classroom have evolved dramatically to include a host of active-learning opportunities for students. Faculty at Eastern Kentucky University (EKU) strive to engage students and offer them a learner-centered environment where they develop and reinforce skill sets, using content from all courses to assist their success in life, beyond academics and the classroom. In addition, faculty engage in professional development through presentations in the Teaching & Learning Innovation (TLI) series, explore and complete online classes on innovative pedagogical strategies from our selection of DEEP (Developing Excellence in Eastern's Professors) courses, and use lessons learned in and out of their classes to make learning an active process that yields results. As Felder (2011) wrote,

> Learner-centered methods have repeatedly been shown to be superior to the traditional teacher-centered approach to instruction, a conclusion that applies whether the assessed outcome is short-term mastery, long-term retention, or depth of understanding of course material, acquisition of critical thinking or creative problem-solving skills, formation of positive attitudes toward the subject being taught, or level of self-confidence in knowledge and skills. (n.p)

Weimer (2012) has outlined five characteristics of learner-centered teaching and proposes that students should be involved in the messy work of learning. This point echoes the shift from traditional approaches to current trends based on active learning. Weimer also asserts that teachers should explicitly teach skills along with content to provide meaning based on using content to teach students how to do something with it rather than just storing it for assessment. Further, Weimer refers to metacognitive strategies to discuss the need for students to reflect on how and what they learn. Learner-centered approaches provide the motivation students need to feel like agents in their learning.

As we become more explicit about what students are learning and why it is valuable, learners are more willing to engage. We can earn more buy-in from learners as we become more transparent about learning. As we focus on the learner, we must help them to be aware of their learning process for, as Mulnix explained, "a challenge in achieving transparency is developing a deep awareness of our own processes. Only then can we explicitly teach those thinking processes" (n.p.)

Blum (2016) has written on learning versus schooling and offers valuable insights on the importance of deconstructing the confines of "school" to encourage learning. She acknowledges there is no unique way to go about this, but "there are a few approaches that could improve learning: more fun, curiosity, connection, usefulness, amazement; less emphasis on control and measurement; a greater sense of shared enterprise among all of us; and less regard for education as a zero-sum *game*" (Blum). If learning is not the center, then students concentrate on what she calls the "game" of amassing points and checking boxes without full engagement. With a focus on the learner, though, we must also go beyond pure pedagogical strategy and meet students where they are. Today's student faces many challenges that can put them at risk during their college career. We see students who come from poverty, toxic stress, trauma, abuse, and other factors that impact their ability to succeed. In her book *Breakaway Learners*, Gross (2017) addressed those issues and uses her term "lasticity" as a cornerstone to bridging the achievement gap. For Gross, lasticity is "is grounded in psychology, neuroscience, sociology, education, trauma theory and moral philosophy" (n.p.). This concept is largely based on reciprocity whereby instructors provide a "shoulder to learn on." Because of our commitment to learner-centered teaching, it was logical to make student-centered teaching and learning the theme of the 2018 Pedagogicon held at Crabbe Library on EKU's campus focused on student-centered teaching and learning. Presenters showed us how they provide a shoulder to learn on through innovative pedagogy. This congregation of pedagogues did not disappoint as they shared lessons learned in a way that engaged participants in active learning processes.

The collection of manuscripts represented here is the culmination of lessons shared at the 2018 Pedagogicon and targets some of the main themes of learner-centered teaching. We have essays on metacognitive processes, which serve as reminders that we must show students to reflect on what and how they learn. A focus on metacognition also allows for work on critical reading and thinking thereby explicitly teaching skills along with content. Here at EKU, we have implemented research on metacognition as we scale the institution's Quality Enhancement Plan (QEP) of critical reading.

Student engagement was another theme that pervaded the presentations. With a focus on the learner, tips on how to engage students are critical. The theme of student engagement extended to work on the reciprocity (much like Blum suggests) as we look at students as teachers and teachers as students. The learning process is not a unilateral one. Rather, it is based on reciprocity and collaboration. Finally, we recognized work on new technologies and emerging trends. We have the tools we need to make learning synchronous and collaborative in online and face to face courses. Learning is not something that occurs most fruitfully in isolation, so we have included tips on how to best implement technology to keep the focus on the learner across course delivery formats.

The integration of student-centered learning can take many forms. We have countless options on how to make learning meaningful and develop assessment tools that help learners and teachers know when deep learning is occurring. In the articles that follow, authors provide valuable insights about putting the learner first. The articles offer fresh perspectives about learners and show us how important the focus on the learner is. It is also a good reminder that teachers are learners too. From this volume, the editors hope you gain insights about strategies to improve the learner's experience and keep on learning! We hope you enjoy the exciting collection of tips to keep the focus of your classes on the learners. May this collection help you to be the shoulder for your students to learn on.

Weimer (2012) outlines five characteristics of learner-centered teaching. She asserts that students are not always as involved in the messy work of learning as they should be. Instructors often call the shots in the classroom. They ask the questions, call on students, and elaborate to make points. While all of this is important in the right doses, it can be too much and thus take away some of the practice time for students thereby limiting their deep learning. Instead of preparing lectures and asking all the questions, instructors might opt to prepare inquiry and subsequent discussion so that the students are challenging one another, elaborating on points made and engaging in the learning process.

Second, Weimer calls for explicit skill instruction whereby students learn to think, create, and apply knowledge of the content. Skills are transferable and help to fill the toolkit students will take when they leave university and move toward their professional lives. Whether we are dealing with hard sciences or humanities courses, we can offer students a space for experimentation where they read and think critically to solve problems relating to their content and discipline.

Third, Weimer reminds us that learners should reflect on what they learn and how they learn it. Thinking about how we learn and what we retain uses metacognitive strategies and aids in deep learning as well as the articulation of lessons learned. Not only can learners use their learning in real contexts, they can be mindful of what they have learned and articulate knowledge. We do not simply want learners to know facts, we strive to help them achieve the skills they need to use those facts.

Weimer encourages learner-centered approaches for motivating students as well. If students have some control in the learning process, they see themselves as agents. This agency passed on to students also allows them to have an increased sense of community. As students take charge of their learning, they collaborate and become capable of sharing lessons with peers and teachers. The teacher has expertise in content areas, but learners have valuable lessons to share as well. This sort of collaboration helps to create a learning space where learners feel comfortable and empowered to practice and engage.

As faculty engage learners, several other goals are achieved. We are employing principles of high impact practices in our classrooms which lead to deep learning and make assessment of learning more informative. In Weimer's remarks on community building, she echoes some of Kuh's (2008) work on high impact practices. This is especially noted in the reference to collaboration. If instructors are carefully crafting the class activities, learners are involved in common intellectual experiences, collaborative assignments and projects and learning communities. By approaching classes as opportunities for enrichment through common intellectual experiences, it is natural to implement collaboration in assignments that might be completed in or out of class. With these practices in the classroom, learning communities are created. Of course, those learning communities can extend to other areas like living quarters and campus wide activities.

As we focus on the learner, the implementation of new pedagogical strategies is a natural progression. By integrating community and active learning, we can improve courses in all formats. We have the technology we need to make online courses interactive and provide occasions for synchronous learning. We are not limited to learners engaging in learning in isolation. Flipping our classes, using appropriate technology, using assessment meaningfully and getting students involved in their communities both here and abroad help better prepare students for the world in which they live. They should be able to face diversity in terms of learning and being culturally competent through an understanding of self and other.

2018 CFP and Theme

The theme of the 2018 Pedagogicon was student-centered teaching and learning. The call for proposals invited scholars from across the Commonwealth and country to share and examine those practices that have proven highly effective in engaging students in learning; that is, student-centered teaching and learning. Presenters–and now authors discuss theories and practices of student-centered teaching and learning broadly and in practice in their classrooms.

Metacognition

In "Using Metacognitive Microactivities to Engage Students," Wren Mills defines metacognition and describes microactivities along with how they can be integrated into both in-person and online courses. Next, in "Critical Reading Skills of Graduate Occupational Therapy Students: A Scholarship of Teaching and Learning Project," Leslie J. Hardman and MaryEllen Thompson introduce a scholarship of teaching and learning (SoTL) project that they completed with occupational therapy (OT) students to assess and improve critical reading skills in a graduate course. James McClure, in "Creative Writing as Queer Process Pedagogy in the Straight-Aligned Post-Secondary Composition Classroom," explains how using creative writing course techniques during the composition process, queer and straight students alike will be able to become more effective communicators together. Shirley Peganoff O'Brien and Camille Skubik-Peplaski, in "Metacognition: Using Critical Reading Strategies to Promote Critical Thinking and Clinical Reasoning," explore the use of effortful learning and focused feedback about critical reading techniques. Students in their study were able to actively engage in preparation for professional reasoning in occupational therapy practice. In "Student Perception of Mindfulness Strategies' Impact on Student Learning," Jennifer Hight explores the effects of mindfulness implementation in the college classroom to understand student metacognition and perceptions of using mindfulness to promote learning.

New Technologies and Emerging Trends

In the New Technologies and Emerging Trends section, authors propose unique ideas on how to use technologies to get students active and interactive. Thad Crews uses a data-driven approach to assessing student perceptions of learning and their preferences to help gauge how teaching can best come from three dimensions. That is, Crews implements a multi-faceted approach to class time and content delivery. Jason P. Johnston, Diane N. Loeffler and Blake L. Jones discuss the use of podcasts for active learning. They explain how podcasts allow interaction in the completion of assignments with the ease of portability and specialized instruction.

Podcasts, as the authors note, are a great medium for inter(action) inside and outside the classroom. Firm Faith Watson discusses planning an online course through backward design to allow for deeper learning. Watson explains how the assessments of the course become more meaningful when they are thoroughly considered in the design phase of an online course. April R. Hatcher and Sara B. Police show how the Jigsaw method and Virtual Field Trips (VFTs) can work effectively in unexpected places. Their study shows how mixing VFTs and the jigsaw method allowed for an effective course assignment in a graduate level nutrition course. Finally in this section, Lesia Lennex and Justin Elswick discuss the effective implementation of Makerspaces and 3D printing to craft assignments for varying levels of learners. Readers are sure to gain fresh ideas on how to integrate new technologies into their courses for a refresh of traditional assignments that will get students involved in active learning.

Student Engagement

In the Student Engagement section, the authors examine strategies for designing effective teaching environments for learning. In "Adjusting Teaching Practices to Benefit Generation Z Learners," Gaby Bedetti argues that a current practice contributing to student-centered learning, especially deep learning, is to target students' learning styles. As described in this contribution, Bedetti surveyed an upper-level literature class to determine the students' preferred learning styles. In "Reinventing Student Engagement: The Role of In-class Simulation," Keri New, Catherine Edwards, Shannon Shumaker, and Brooke Bentley explore classroom simulation and debriefing to provide learners an opportunity to integrate didactic content into various clinical situations. As the authors argue, this type of pedagogy allows students to critically think and apply decision-making skills within a controlled, interactive environment. Michelle A. Gremp, in "Team-Based Learning: An Opportunity to Model Student-Centered Learning in a Teacher Preparation Course," explains that quality post-secondary instruction should move beyond merely covering content to providing authentic opportunities for students. Gremp offers team-based learning as a pedagogical approach that models student-centered learning. In "Best Practices for Engaging Introverts," Susan Weaver, Glenda Warren, and Chris Lockhart offer strategies to provide introverts with the privacy and control that they need for success. They also provide a set of recommendations to help all students learn about individual differences. Melony A. Shemberger, in "Going Back in Time: Designing Student Learning Through Oral History Interviews," shares lessons from projects in two journalism and mass communications courses.

Teachers as Students, Students as Teachers

In "First Steps in Qualitative Research," Aimee M. Cloutier and Ella L. Ingram introduce core components of high-quality qualitative research as a foundation for scholars. They reflect on the perspectives brought to the study of qualitative research and their experience with a faculty development program that introduced qualitative research to STEM faculty. Lynda N. Donathan and Anthony T. Dotson, in "Incorporating Soft Skills for Student Success," argue that it is important to identify essential soft skills inside and outside of the classroom and ways to incorporate these skills. The authors then reinforce how a focus on soft skills in professional education can influence success in today's workplace. In "Engaging Agents: Students as Class Facilitators for Academic Articles," Tanya Robertson encourages instructors to consider using students, agents, as class facilitators to teach academic articles. Jessica Vaught introduces the use of zines as alternative assessment in course assignments in her work entitled "Resistive Pedagogy: Student-Facilitated Learning and Literacy through Zines." In the final contribution to this section, John Strada, Krista M. Kimmel, and Jennifer L. Fairchild, in "Using Assessment Data to Create Targeted Instructor Training," discuss the implications for a basic communication course training program based on a university-mandated, biennial general education assessment of basic course speech assignments during. This section brings the reader full circle in considerations of teaching practices based upon research models, to key considerations in course design and student roles to the outcome evaluation of programmatic curriculum work.

Discussion

Student-centered approaches foster success in the classroom. When lessons are designed to include active learning, collaboration, and inquery, deep learning is more likely to occur. At Eastern Kentucky University, we strive to prepare our students for success in the classroom by community building and an inclusion of all students and all approaches to learning. Professional development opportunities are organized to offer instructors time and community to consider the implementation of new pedagogical strategies. Those efforts often culminate in presentations during Scholars Week and participation in events such as the Pedagogicon.

Recommendations

The wide range of topics addressed in the volume serve as reminders of how we can keep our focus on the students. In order to effectively engage students, we must first realize who our students are taking into account their assets and challenges. This approach can help us meet them where they are, create a positive learning environment, and see them become active and engaged learners. The classroom is usually where we start with our commitment to students, but it is also important to help them see how to apply their learning to real situations. Providing them opportunity to learn outside the classroom through activities linked to course content, service learning, study abroad, and internships to name a few are critical. As students take multiple paths to learning, they become more confident and are better positioned to engage in metacognitive learning moments. Thus, as facilitators of learning, we should seek student input often and continually seek innovative ways to empower student learning by:
- Focusing on learning in (and outside) of the classroom,
- Starting where students are,
- Inviting student input often,
- Reducing barriers to learning for students, and
- Creating metacognitive learning moments and environments.

References

Blum, S. D. (2015, December 28). Learning vs school. [Blog post]. Retrieved from http://www.susanblum.com/learning-versus-schooling-a-blog-about-both/the-game-of-school

Felder, R. M. (n.d.). Learner-centered teaching. Retrieved from http://www4.ncsu.edu/unity/lockers/users/f/felder/public//Student-Centered.html

Gross, K. (2017). *Breakaway learners: Strategies for post-secondary success with at-risk students.* New York, NY: Teachers College Press.

Kuh, G. (2008). High-impact educational practices: A brief overview. Retrieved from https://www.aacu.org/leap/hips

Mulnix, A. B. (2016). The power of transparency in your teaching. *Faculty Focus.* Retrieved from https://www.facultyfocus.com/articles/course-design-ideas/power-transparency-teaching/

Weimer, M. (2012). Five characteristics of learner-centered teaching. *Faculty Focus.* Retrieved from https://www.facultyfocus.com/articles/effective-teaching-strategies/five-characteristics-of-learner-centered-teaching/

Acknowledgements

The editors wish to thank the authors of the 2018 proceedings of the Pedagogicon for their dedication to seeking and sharing innovative approaches to teaching and learning. Thank you to the many excellent presenters at the 2018 conference for sharing their scholarship of teaching and learning with us and allowing us to learn from their innovative and inspiring work. We wish to acknowledge the Faculty Innovators at EKU for their commitment to the enhancement of teaching, learning, and faculty development across campus. Finally, we wish to acknowledge our sincere appreciation to our colleagues and friends in the Crabbe Library, Noel Studio for Academic Creativity, and Faculty Center for Teaching & Learning for providing inspiring and creative spaces within which to coordinate innovative teaching and learning efforts such as the annual Pedagogicon.

Using Metacognitive Microactivities to Engage Students

Wren Mills
Western Kentucky University

The sage-on-the-stage teaching model is outdated and seldom an effective method for teaching today's learners. However, many faculty struggle with giving up that kind of control over their classes—both in person and online—or are unsure of how to break up lectures or what kinds of activities to put in place to help students to learn more effectively. This paper reviews key ideas from the books Visible Learning and the Science of How We Learn, Make It Stick, *and* Small Teaching *in addition to a paper presented at the National Institute on the Teaching of Psychology. This paper will define metacognition and describe microactivities before discussing how they can be integrated into both in-person and online courses. The recommendation to instructors is to incorporate at least one microactivity each week if not each class period.*

Introduction

As higher education has moved toward a more student-centered, active and applied learning focus, the sage-on-the-stage model is no longer seen as the most effective method for teaching. However, many faculty struggle with giving up that control of their classes—both in person and online—or are unsure of how to break up or replace lectures or what kinds of activities to put in their place to help students to learn most effectively. Ideas from the books *Visible Learning and the Science of How We Learn* (Hattie & Yates, 2014), *Make it Stick* (Brown, Roediger, & McDaniel, 2014), and *Small Teaching* (Lang, 2016), help us to understand how the brain works when it comes to learning and what types of activities are most effective at helping us learn.

Research and Rationale

Metacognition is uttered so often in education today that it might seem like a buzzword, a trend that will come and go, but it is essential for learning and student success. Because of this, it is important to be clear on the definition of metacognition, which Merriam-Webster defines as "awareness or analysis of one's own learning or thinking processes," or as some put it, "thinking about thinking," and it is key to how the brain learns new ideas and commits them to memory.

In their chapter "How Knowledge is Acquired," Hattie and Yates (2014) shared that learners have to "touch" information multiple times, and preferably in different ways, before they can move it from short-term to long-term memory. They identified and discussed three steps to true learning. First, information is introduced, and the brain will retain that for 5-20 seconds before the ideas start to fade if they are not revisited quickly. When the material is revisited immediately, the brain begins to make connections, and the move of the information toward long-term memory begins. For example, when the instructor mentions a new term, if it is just stated and maybe defined, but then the lecturer moves on, chances are that the learners will not retain that term or its definition. However, if the lecturer gives examples and explanations of the term, ties the term to prior learning in the course or asks students to consider their past interactions with the concept, and then introduces an activity or assignment that has students apply the material, students are far more likely to remember the ideas beyond the class period.

These points about the mechanics of how the brain learns are furthered by Hattie and Yates's (2014) stipulation that learners need "…time, goal-orientation, supportive feedback, accumulated successful practice, and frequent review" to achieve meaningful learning (p. 113). James Lang (2016) reiterated these points in *Small Teaching*, where he recommended small activities and assignments that encourage retrieval, predicting, practice, and interleaving with past knowledge and prior experiences among other types of activities to promote learning. Brown, Roediger, and McDaniel (2014) echoed that the best learning happens when opportunities are spaced out and allow for "elaboration" (p. 4), which deepens learning and expands the brain's "capacity" (p. 5).

This approach is obviously different from a traditional lecture-format course. Instructors should provide students with a chance to struggle with the material and make sense of it, with the former encouraging deeper learning via multiple active learning opportunities. As Brown, Roediger, and McDaniel (2014) said in *Make it Stick,* "...effortful learning changes the brain" (p. 199). This means students must practice, revisit, and work more with new concepts to learn best.

Additionally, Hattie and Yates (2014) reminded readers that the attention span of the average person is around 12-15 minutes, which has implications for the sage-on-the-stage model. Rather than an hour or more of straight lecturing, faculty need to "chunk" the information in their lectures so that they can reset their students' attention spans and keep them attuned to what is being said and allow them to appropriately process and practice using and applying the information. Couple this with the primacy (what is heard first) and recency (what is heard last) effects, and faculty will realize that information covered in the middle of a lecture is more likely to get lost in the mix (Hattie & Yates). Last, instructors should also consider the attention span limits and primacy and recency effect with Lang's (2016) suggestion that learning new materials or skills within a single long session is less effective than practicing and learning over several spaced shorter sessions, a point that Hattie and Yates (2014) as well as Brown, Roediger, and McDaniel (2014) also made.

With these ideas in mind—presenting and using information in multiple ways, breaking every 12-15 minutes of lecture to reset attention spans and actively use the information acquired, and the need to revisit information from the middle of a lecture more than what was at the start or end of it— Amy Marin's (2011) "Mindful Moments" activities become prime candidates for easy integration into most courses (online here: https://docs.google.com/file/d/0B1ERChsMmczqbDhvM3p0Vi04OTQ/edit). While these activities are written for in-person psychology classes, they are easily adaptable for most disciplines and any class format. They are meant to be quick metacognitive check-ins for students to pause, retrieve and use information, and to have a chance to quickly ask questions before instructors continue on with the lesson or lecture. With the immediate feedback students will receive from both their instructor and their peers, both instructor and student will be able to gauge if the material is being absorbed or if it needs to be revisited before moving on to new ideas. These activities help students "know what they don't know." Ideally, each microactivity will last fewer than 5 minutes, but most of Marin's ideas can be expanded to last longer. Marin shared 50 of them, so instructors can pick and choose those that best align with daily, weekly, and course learning objectives and fit the needs of the lesson—both those of the content and those of the instructor's and the class's personality.

How to Implement
Using in In-person Classes

The beauty of microactivities is that instructors can use them at any point in any class as long as they are helping students to work with material. The most common ways to integrate them into an in-person class are to get the class started, to break up lectures and reset the attention span of students, and to close a lesson.

For example, at the start of class, if a new topic is being introduced, have students pair up and do a "Brainstorm Blitz" to get them pondering possible meanings, points to be covered, expectations about the topics, and even help the instructor to see misconceptions that are arising in addition to seeing what students' prior knowledge about that topic is (Marin, 2011). After 15-20 minutes of lecture, the instructor might pause and have students do an application activity. For example, if the topic is one that is relevant to many fields, a "Who can use it?" activity would have students brainstorm how workers across disciplines might use that concept in their daily work (Marin). If the topic being covered is a bit technical or involves a process, students could be asked to participate in an "Active Listening" activity, where one students has to explain the concept while the other notes what is correct or not, and then they switch positions to make sure they can both explain it—or realize that they cannot and ask for help or clarification (Marin). A third very popular quick reset activity is to give students a couple of minutes to "Check Your Notes" against those of the people around them, and then allow a couple of minutes to clarify any points which the students could not sort out themselves (Marin). Instructors should keep in mind with these activities the primacy and recency effects: since students are most likely to "forget" what is in the middle of the lecture, giving them topics to work with from that segment may be most beneficial to their learning.

To close the day's lesson, students could be asked to create a "Graphic Organizer" of that day's notes (2-3 minutes), and then asked to share with 1-2 other students around them (2-3 minutes) to see if they all have the same information organized in the same way (Marin, 2011). Instructors should leave time for questions in case students find differences that they are unable to resolve amongst themselves. If an exit ticket approach is preferred, a "Rose and Thorn" paper could be completed, which allows students to share with the instructor which ideas were most interesting and most confusing (Marin).

A final example of an activity that includes both the start and end of class is to do a popular "Bookend" activity (Marin, 2011). At the start of class, students predict what will be learned about that day's topic or perhaps how it fits in to the larger unit or the course as a whole. At the end of class, students return to their predictions and write corrections if needed and reflect on why they were or were not correct in their prediction. Reflections are an important part of metacognition, as they embody the concept of "thinking about thinking" and can help students to consider important connections among material that they otherwise might not.

Using in Online Classes

Many of the activities can be adapted for use in online courses with video lectures or via a tool like Blackboard's Adaptive Release (students cannot proceed in an online lesson until they complete a task to unlock the next in the series). A sample lesson in an online course could start with an overall lesson discussion board, setting it so that students cannot see others' posts until they make their own with their ideas about the topic, and then they have to respond to at least one other student to trigger the adaptive release to open the lecture for the unit. Just as in an in-person class, the first activity could be a "Brainstorm Blitz," where students would post their answers to a prompt and then respond to 1-2 other students' answers, and then the video lecture link for the lesson would open for them to watch. Note that this helps discussions to be engaging, active learning opportunities where students receive feedback fairly quickly on their ideas, if not immediately by seeing other students' responses, just as they would in an in-person classroom.

Next, the video lecture can either be broken into multiple parts with the microactivities built in between each one, or the lecturer can simply say, "Please pause the video now, and complete the 'Who can use it' activity before resuming the video." Students could be referred back to the discussion board for that activity, or instead they might complete a quick quiz or assignment for instructor-only feedback. The final activity of the in-class lesson—a "Graphic Organizer"— either can be posted on the lesson discussion board for peer and instructor feedback, or submitted for instructor-only feedback in an online class.

Considerations for Putting Ideas into Practice

Just as with other learning activities and assignments, microactivities should be planned thoughtfully for best integration. What follows are a few suggestions for best implementation:

1. Remember Alignment: All activities and assessments in a course should point back toward–or *align with*–at least one of the course or unit/daily objectives.
2. While students appreciate variety and "mixing things up," they (and instructors) will be much happier if instructors find just a few microactivities to use through the semester. This ends up being a time-saver, too. While the instructor will have to explain how to do each activity the first time it is used, after that, students can be told, "Okay! Let's do a 'Brainstorm Blitz!'" and they will know exactly what to do, thus helping to keep the lesson moving.
3. Practice each microactivity before taking it into the classroom. Knowing how to explain the activity to students (especially the first time) is key to its going well. It is also recommended

to do a test run of it with student workers, colleagues, or friends/family to make sure no steps or instructions are being omitted.
4. While many microactivities are easy to draft in just minutes, some take planning. Make sure all of the materials needed are on hand. For example, one requires a beach ball, and many require sticky notes or other easily obtained but vital materials that will keep the activity from going smoothly if not brought to class or not easily accessible for your online learners.

Know Your Resources

Most institutions have at least one instructional designer on staff who can help instructors to best design the use of microactivities within their courses. Do not hesitate to seek out this person on campus, as often instructional designers know of tools and tricks for making classes more engaging and methods of implementing metacognitive activities of which instructors are not aware.

Also remember that every campus has faculty who are experienced with active learning both in the classroom and online and are more than happy to share ideas with others. Most institutions have a teaching and learning center on campus, as well, who might be able to connect you with resources or mentors. Be sure to seek out these colleagues to help you get started.

Conclusion

Many instructors who use Marin's (2011) metacognitive activities notice that a lot of them are, well, *fun*. Marin found that students learn better when they are motivated and interested in their learning activities, and with that in mind, some microactivities are game-like. It is not unheard of for these activities to raise the energy level in a classroom, as well, which makes them great for night-classes and other classes that might meet for longer than a typical hour-long session. These activities can be used with students at all levels of learning, from first semester freshmen to graduate students and participants in faculty development workshops and conference sessions have been known to enjoy them. Many instructors appreciate the energy and new levels of learning that they can bring to a class, and hopefully you will, too.

References

Hattie, J., & Yates, G. C. R. (2014). How learning is acquired. In J. Hattie & G. C. R. Yates (Eds.), *Visible learning and the science of how we learn* (pp. 113-125). New York: Routledge.

Lang, J. (2016). *Small teaching: Everyday lessons from the science of learning.* New York: Jossey-Bass.

Marin, A. (2011). *Using active learning to energize the psychology classroom: Fifty exercises that take five minutes or less.* Paper presented at the National Institute on the Teaching of Psychology, St. Petersburg, FL.

Critical Reading Skills of Graduate Occupational Therapy Students: A Scholarship of Teaching and Learning Project

Leslie J. Hardman & MaryEllen Thompson
Eastern Kentucky University

This article introduces a Scholarship of Teaching and Learning (SoTL) project completed with occupational therapy (OT) students to assess and improve critical reading skills in the context of a graduate level course. This mixed methods study looks at student self-rating and self-perceptions of critical reading skills before and after targeted assignments, explicit critical reading instruction, and library instruction. Results examined here suggest graduate students' critical reading skills vary greatly and that students can benefit from explicit instruction. The authors explore project results and discuss limitations as well as information to guide curriculum for the benefit of all students within a professional degree program.

Introduction

Occupational therapy faculty value critical reading as a core skill for graduate occupational therapy student success. There is a paucity of research focused on critical reading skills of occupational therapy students. Similarly, little evidence of scholarship of teaching and learning (SoTL) research has been conducted in this population to inform curricular design or content for student success in critical reading. Burns, Merchant, & Appelt (2013), surveyed health sciences faculty about attitudes and involvement in SoTL. Overall, these faculty found value in SoTL as a means to participate in educational research, develop teaching practices, and support classroom methods. Using examples of their own SoTL research, Manarin, Carey, Rathburn, and Ryland (2015) provide a rationale for explicit teaching of critical reading in higher education and specific strategies to employ for student skill development. Occupational therapy faculty implemented a SoTL project in a graduate occupational therapy course to assess student critical reading before and after explicit instruction and targeted course assignments. Qualitative and quantitative data was collected to discover student competencies in critical reading and student self-perception of their critical reading skills. Project description and discussion of project data follows in hopes of informing graduate student teaching practices related to critical reading.

Program context

Gallo and Rinaldo (2012) contend in their study of undergraduate biology student critical reading styles, the premise that reading and evaluating relevant primary literature is imperative to one's development as a scientist (during and after degree completion). Agreeing with this example, two faculty in a secondary public university Master of Occupational Therapy program, identified expectations for students to have competency in critical reading skills for peer-reviewed literature, which includes scientific literature. This literature is assigned reading in addition to course textbooks in all graduate course work. Course expectations include reading, understanding, evaluation, application and synthesis of text book reading and peer reviewed professional literature. Faculty believe reading and using current, research based literature is key to development of clinical knowledge and professional skills as a future occupational therapist.
Faculty further identified:
- Students often not reading or re-reading assigned literature (Nilson, 2010).

- Students not understanding what they read.
- Students' poor application of the literature content in written or laboratory assignments.
- Students' critical reading skills not clearly defined.
- Faculty expectation of students not clearly defined (Paul & Elder, 2005).
- Student expectations of assigned reading not clearly defined.

To support faculty assumptions and student expectation, they sought to understand student critical reading skill levels and to identify the tools needed to improve their skills. Prior to the development of this SoTL project, faculty participated in a critical reading professional learning community, 2017. This supported their commitment to develop a process to assess student critical reading skills, teach/equip them with strategies and tools, and reassess skills to assure learning.

Project approach/project overview

Occupational therapy faculty implemented an SoTL project in three sections of a graduate occupational therapy course (n=77), spring 2018. The course, OTS 824 Health Care Practice II, taught in three sections, includes intensive pediatric theory and lab work and is foundational for occupational therapy practice upon degree completion. This is in the second semester of a master of occupational therapy program.

The project questions included: Does the use of explicitly taught critical reading (CR) strategies improve student critical reading skills? Do students using specific critical reading strategies perceive improved understanding and application of journal reading?

Faculty designed a mixed methods project. During weeks one and six, students completed a purposeful reading assignment (PR) and a student survey of their perceived critical reading skills. The PR assignments were graded by two faculty using an adaptation of their university's critical reading rubric. Rubric scores were assigned as beginning (0), developing (1), competent (2), or accomplished (3) for each of four defined categories/concepts (comprehension, analysis, synthesis, and evaluation) and up to one point each for timeliness, length of assignment response and spelling/grammar (Maximum possible score =15). Each of two faculty independently graded each (n=77) student assignment, then reviewed the scores and criteria, arriving at the final score for each student by consensus. The PR grades and student survey scores constitute the quantitative data. Student open-ended self-perception survey questions on the second survey constitutes the project qualitative data.

Although the PR assignment is a project tool for data collection, the assignment itself serves as critical reading tool; guiding students to derive meaning from the text and ask questions of the text. (Van Gyn, 2013; Tomesek, 2009). The journal articles selected by faculty were specific to course content for weeks one and six (DeGrace, Foust, Sisson, & Lora, 2016; Fingerhut, Piro, Sutton, Campbell, Lewis, Lawji, & Martinez, 2013). Intervention during weeks two through five included in class review of the first PR assignment and grading, expectations for the second PR assignment, explicit critical reading instruction and library instruction occurring before the second PR assignment. Students participated in one session of explicit critical reading instruction (Bosley & Parrot, 2013). Faculty modeled critical reading strategies in class and provided written instruction for critical reading strategies. One library instruction session was conducted for all students. This library session emphasized the information literacy concepts of 1. Authority is Constructed and Contextual and 2. Scholarship as Conversation (American Library Association, 2015). Faculty reinforced the importance of noting the authors and their context and well as questioning the authors and the the literature content as important to understanding the relevance and significance of a text. Faculty further reinforced application of the literature content to course context.

In week six, students completed a second PR assignment, repeating the quantitative student survey and a first time qualitative questionnaire. Student assignment grades and pre and post surveys are compared for presence of or lack of meaningful changes in targeted critical reading skills and student self-perception of critical reading skills.

Analysis

On the first purposeful reading assignment (prior to intervention), disparate student skills on a scale, beginning to accomplished, were noted for evaluation of author and article authority as well as synthesis of the peer reviewed text significant concepts. The majority of students were competent or accomplished for comprehension, defined as answering 75% or more of the factual question(s) about the text. This suggests students initially command skills to search text for facts but are inconsistent for skills to question, challenge, and synthesize text content beyond the facts.

From the final quantitative data analysis, student total change scores on the purposeful reading assignments indicates significance for a score increase; 45.5% of students (n=77), no change 19.5%, and decrease 35%. There was also an overall student score increase in specific critical reading rubric categories of comprehension and evaluation. From the student critical reading survey, pre/post change scores showing an increase are most significant for the following questions: #5, "I can determine the authority of the text author(s)" and #7, "I use critical reading strategies to help me understand texts."

From the qualitative analysis, student written responses show perceived improved competence with understanding purpose of the text, determining authority of text author and using critical reading strategies. They specifically identified the meaningfulness of the critical reading instruction and the importance of library instruction. Interestingly, students also identified a desire to continue access to library resources for professional peer reviewed literature beyond their course requirements in the future.

The project is deemed a success based on pre/post change scores on the purposeful reading assignments and the student surveys. The SoTL process supported faculty to closely analyze critical reading expectations for students, inform course critical reading instruction, and guide assignment/curricular design going forward. Discussion of the limitations of this project and potential redesign for future SoTL projects for the benefit of the students to meet learning objectives is beneficial.

Discussion and Considerations

The SoTL project allowed faculty to assess and guide graduate student critical reading skills in the context of the classroom. The purposeful reading (PR) assignments were themselves critical reading teaching tools. As faculty analyzed the process and data, it is determined that PR assignments could be used as a tool at regular intervals, i.e. per semester or per year, to establish student baseline of critical reading skills and to measure progress. These measures can inform targeted student course instruction and curricular content.

In the project, the second PR assignment grading was delayed in comparison to the first. Feedback for this assignment occurred after week six and the second student critical reading survey. Per student feedback and faculty assessment it would be beneficial to give immediate PR assignment feedback for maximum benefit to the student.

Students also gave feedback indicating they wanted more review of PR assignment expectations and detailed explanation of the critical reading grading rubric. They went on to indicate a desire for faculty to state critical reading expectations for all course assignments. Related to library instruction, students overall found value in the session. Many stated there was redundancy from previous library instruction from undergraduate and graduate courses. This informs faculty to communicate about library instruction across the curriculum and work to scaffold library instruction content. It would follow that faculty collaboration across the curriculum, not just in one course, is necessary to embed critical reading assessment/reassessment, instruction, and course design for student critical reading skill development. Opportunities for faculty as informed by the SoTL project include increasing explicit critical reading instruction throughout the course as well as faculty modeling of critical reading strategies with textbook reading and other course materials.

Limitations noted by faculty further include that some students PR assignment decreased total scores may have resulted from timing of the second assignment (week six) when their total course load demands are high nearing midterm; also some students indicated not valuing the assignment as they perceived self as competent in critical reading skills. Faculty also noted the PR assignment score was established as low stakes within the student's total semester grade which could impact if the student valued the assignment enough to give their best effort on the first and/or second opportunity.

The SoTL project proved to challenge the faculty and the students to examine student critical reading skills specific to peer reviewed journal literature. Students within the targeted graduate course demonstrate a wide range of critical reading skills, perceive their critical reading skills differently than faculty and demonstrate a desire to engage with literature in a meaningful way for their course completion and future professions. The challenge to faculty moving forward is to accurately assess, and reassess, student critical reading skills across the curriculum and model effective critical reading strategies for student success.

References

American Library Association. (2015). Framework for information literacy for higher education. http://www.ala.org/acrl/standards/ilframework. Retrieved 10/12/17.

Bishop-Clark, C., & Dietz-Uhler, B. (2012). *Engaging in the scholarship of teaching and learning.* Sterling, VA: Stylus Publishing.

Bosley, L., & Parrott, J. (2013). Developing critical readers through metacognitive strategies. EKU Teaching and Learning Series.

Burns, S., Merchant, C., & Appelt, E. (2013). Campus survey on the status of the scholarship of teaching and learning (SoTL) by health sciences faculty. *Education, 133*(4), 502-512.

*DeGrace, B. W., Foust, R. E., Sisson, S. B., & Lora, K. R. (2016). Brief Report—Benefits of family meals for children with special therapeutic and behavioral needs. *American Journal of Occupational Therapy, 70,* 7003350010. http://dx.doi.org/10.5014/ajot.2016.014969

*Fingerhut, P. E., Piro, J., Sutton, A., Campbell, R., Lewis C., Lawji, D., & Martinez, N. (2013). Family-centered principles implemented in home-based, clinic-based, and school-based settings. *American Journal of Occupational Therapy, 67,* 228-235.

Gallo, M., & Rinaldo, V. (2012). Towards a mastery understanding of critical reading in biology: The use of highlighting by students to assess their value judgment of the importance of primary literature. *Journal of Microbiology & Biology Education: JMBE, 13*(2), 142–149. http://doi.org/10.1128/jmbe.v13i2.493

Manarin, K., Carey, M., Rathburn, M., & Ryland, G. (2015). *Using critical reading in higher education academic goals and social engagement.* Bloomington, IN: Indiana University Press.

Nilson, L. B. (2010). Getting Students to do the Readings. In *Teaching at its best: A research-based resource for college instructors* (pp. 211-222) (3rd ed.). San Francisco, CA: Jossey-Bass.

Paul, R. & Elder, L. (2005). *A guide for educators to critical thinking competency standards.* Foundation for critical thinking. Retrieved from http://www.criticalthinking.org/resources/PDF/CT-competencies%202005.pdf

Tomesek, T. (2009). Critical reading: Using reading prompts to promote active engagement with text. *International Journal of Teaching and Learning in Higher Education, 21*(1), 127-132.

Van Gyn, G. (2013). The little assignment with the big impact: Reading, writing, critical reflection, and meaningful discussion. *Faculty Focus.* Retrieved from http://www.facultyfocus.com/articles/instructional-design/the-little-assignment-with-the-big-impact-reading-writing-critical-reflection-and-meaningful-discussion/

* indicates articles used in purposeful reading assignments.

2018 Pedagogicon Proceedings

Copyright © 2018, New Forums Press, Inc., P.O. Box 876, Stillwater, OK 74076. All Rights Reserved.

Creative Writing as Queer Process Pedagogy in the Straight-Aligned Post-Secondary Composition Classroom

James McClure
Eastern Kentucky University

As the future of the composition classroom moves towards multimodality to redefine academic writing, queer students are still navigating the classroom by appropriating straight-aligned process techniques. By using creative writing course techniques during the composition process, queer and straight students alike will be able to become more effective communicators together.

Introduction

As an undergraduate English student concentrating in creative writing at Eastern Kentucky University (EKU), my college education was focused around studying effective communication through self-expression. In each of my creative writing courses, content production was managed not through secondary research, but through navigating the self to dictate the meaning behind emotion, expression, and intent. Form held a vital role in the creative writing discipline as understanding the characteristics of structure and genre built the foundation of each course.

During this undergraduate study, I enrolled in courses from EKU's graduate school of English to earn both undergraduate credit towards my creative writing degree and graduate credit towards master's degree in composition and rhetoric. In those graduate courses, I noticed that my practice in self-navigation from my creative writing courses helped me think critically about graduate-level research and texts and helped me forfeit my biases when writing in graduate-level discussion. Additionally, the graduate courses helped me approach that self-navigated source material in creative writing with the same critical thinking skills used in reading graduate-level texts. As my liminal experience between undergraduate and graduate studies converged, it became clear that composing under any discipline was symbiotic between self-expression and critical thinking. I argue that employing this symbiosis in the first-year composition (FYC) classroom will help students learn how to communicate effectively not only in their academic disciplines but also in their communities and cultures outside of the academy.

Although many people distinguish the creative writing discipline from FYC because of creative writing's self-explorative nature, the two disciplines ask students to articulate themselves clearly to convey meaning. Both disciplines guide students through communicating to an audience though learning the characteristics of form whether that be literary genre or technical, academic discourse. For Pedagogicon 2018, I proposed that FYC students can practice critical thinking and critical reading skills for effective academic composing though in-class creative writing assignments. The in-class assignment I showcased was developed from a writing prompt out of Lynda Barry's "adult activity book" *What It Is* (2008) where students are prompted to write their memory of the car in a form that is "queered."

Institutional Context

The FYC classroom often acts as the gatekeeper for students entering the university. Having strong cultural ties to methods of communication, incoming students from EKU's service region often may feel that FYC, as a required general education course, acts to remove their personal dialects in favor Standard American English (SAE). Yet, EKU

FYC chooses to embrace the differences between discourse communities by using that difference as a platform for learning rather than teaching students SAE without context of their home cultures. According to the Conference on College Composition and Communication position statement on "Students' Right to Their Own Language" (2014), "[teachers] should be wholly immersed in a dialect group other than their own" to become effective educators (p. 22). By incorporating a queer approach to creative writing activities like Barry's (2008) for use in the FYC classroom, instructors may better enhance student engagement with the discourse communities of themselves, their fellow students, their instructors, and those outside of the academy.

Student-Centered, Queer Activity Design

The following is the creative writing prompt modeled after Barry's (2008) prompt I plan on utilizing as a first-year writing instructor to test the effectiveness of what I proposed at Pedagogicon. *What It Is* presents itself as an "adult activity book" to help people become more creative and artistic thinkers. This prompt asks students to explore their personal spatial positionality to their own memory to create a more expansive, creative, and imagistic expression of that memory.

To participate in the activity, students are asked to "make a list of the first 10 cars that come to [them] from early on in [their] life" and "choose one that seems vivid" (Barry, 2008, p. 143). From there, the students draw a chart separating a sheet of paper into six sections and fill out each of the six sections with the following prompts: put yourself in the vivid image of the car; what is (1) above you, (2) in front of you, (3) to your left, (4) to your right, (5) behind you, and (6) below you (Barry, 2008, p. 153)?

Barry's activity is written through composite images and collage that incorporate text and image in a way that evokes the emotions associated with writing down visual memory (i.e., nostalgia, confusion, and intrigue) and, therefore, acts as a queered text. In addition, the chart the students draw is designed not to function as a list of positionalities concerning the memory but as a composed spatial representation of the position. As they write, students are not composing from top-to-bottom on the page but rather turning the paper on their desk to suit the different angles of the chart. In this case, the student is exploring how writing can be organized and navigated according to both meaning and representation alongside personal expression. The page no longer dictates the organization of the memory, but the memory is now dictating the structure of the page. It is this shift in structure that identifies the in-class assignment as queer.

This act of creative writing against a norm is a form of queer composition that reflects queer studies not in only in composition but in critical thinking. Alexander and Rhodes (2011) write that queer composition is "valuing works that unsettle us, and inviting students to unsettle us with their own formal, stylistic, and content-rich experimentations and improvisations. . . It is recognizing the logic of the impossible" (p. 201). This "logic of the impossible" is the idea that queer composition cannot exist because the idea of "queer" can only exist as a modification of a norm. So, by developing a normed queer composition, it is pushing away from the idea of what makes the composing queer. This is a paradox with the only answer being rhetorical features defined not by form but by self-expression and cultural response.

By breaking standard form, this activity invites students to express and critique beyond the boundaries of the page despite still composing on the page by limiting the students' engagement to only their minds. When asked to write what is left and right in the memory of the car, students are forced to think critically and answer self-directed questions such as: am I inside the car or outside of the car, do I write what I see outside of the window or do I describe the window itself, is there someone with me, and do I describe them? As the students position themselves with their memories as texts to critically read, they understand how their own sight or vision, their own insight or revision, changes how they navigate the text.

This self-awareness is vital to critically reading texts in the FYC classroom; when students are asked to engage with an academic text after creatively writing with this exercise, they are able to navigate the text's meaning and social implication while also responding to it with the same reflective clarity and precision as their own memory. By using their own memories as texts to critically read for this queered form of creative writing, these students are privileging their personal experience in the same way an oppressive classroom privileges a textbook.

By privileging the self through "valuing works that unsettle us," FYC instructors are practicing a more self-reflective critical composing style with their class through creative writing rather than focusing on the form, structure, and genre aspects of creative writing to teach effective communication. As FYC instructors ask students to continue to redefine the boundaries of their comfort zone, they allow their students to grow from positioning the student learning outcomes just outside of that comfort.

Creative Writing as Psychoanalytic Introspection.

When FYC instructors ask students to critically read texts, they are asking students to identify personally their positionality to the texts and their biases concerning the text's form and content before approaching the text critically. This form of self-identification in engagement is considered a psychoanalytic approach rather than an objective approach when Harris (2001) in "Re-Writing the Subject: Psychoanalytic Approaches to Creative Writing and Composition Pedagogy" claims that

> rather than seeing the potential writer as someone who is chameleon-like and changing with each protean discourse he or she adopts, psychoanalysis's more holistic approach enables us to view the individual as a core being whose identity is fluid, mercurial, but self consistent. (p. 185)

This hybrid, liminal identity that students express is the FYC instructors' point of engagement to motivate growth both for the student themselves and for the entire classroom. Reading the self acts as the first step forward in reaching the destination of reading other works with a critical eye. Lunsford (1977) introduced this first step by claiming that "the best way to move students into conceptualization and analytic and synthetic modes of thought is to create assignments and activities which allow students to practice or exercise themselves in these modes continuously," (p. 41) because students are initially "not able to remove themselves from [spontaneous] concepts" (p. 39).

If instructors take this approach of understanding texts and apply it to using the self as a text by using the Barry (2008) activity in the FYC classroom, the students will better contextualize different methods of communication with their respective audiences (Conference on College Composition and Communication, 2014). Students better contextualize the different methods because by creative writing through the queered activity, students are treating themselves and their own minds as the critical texts they read and the audiences they engage with in FYC. The students are literally practicing empathy and engagement with others as they engage with themselves in a queered, creative space.

Barry's Activity as Disorienting FYC Process Pedagogy

Queerness entails forcing people to think critically of how their mind works by using metacognitive strategies to develop a rubric for the self and a set of criteria for self-monitoring, to work to understand their environment to learn how to perform in it, and to compose a sexual and gender identity (Butler, 1988). These conscious, self-monitoring techniques queer people utilize to exist directly correlates to how the FYC classroom asks its students to engage with texts.

Creative writing though Barry's (2008) activity disorients the first-year writing classroom in similar ways a queer identity disorients "the self." By disrupting standardizing methods of classroom function, discussion, and set-up, creative writing exposes the self as a text worthy of rhetorical analysis. But, when that self is queered through navigating it on an obscured form, such as Barry's chart rather than the page, the students analyzing the self creatively are using a set of skills they are asked to learn in FYC: critical thinking, positionality awareness, and effective communication.

By combining creative writing with queer-inspired self-disorienting and self-disruption with Barry's activity, students can practice critically reading and writing simultaneously without the worry of creating a product (e.g. a midterm paper). This emphasis on positional and relative process over objective product aligns with the claims of Murray (2011) who claims that by asking students to write to develop the person rather than develop the product, instructors "must listen carefully for those words that may reveal a truth, that may reveal a voice. We must respect our student for his potential truth and for his potential voice" (p. 5). By focusing on writing to develop a skill rather than develop a component of high-stakes assignment, those queered creative writing activities only exist to benefit the student's ability to (1) think critically inside and outside of the academy, (2) position themselves with the work of others, and (3) respond to the work of others rather than produce products for grading. Though not part of the process of creation, this activity practices the ability to perform these skills needed to engage in any process that requires critical thinking. Therefore, the activity builds the foundation of knowledge from which creative projects can begin.

Discussion and Considerations

Researching the connection between creative writing, queer studies, and FYC for Pedagogicon 2018 served as the beginning of my master's thesis. Upon presenting this research, the response data provided to me asked for more clarity on queer theory and how it relates to creative writing. To build the connection further, I will be exploring more creative writing activities beyond Barry (2008) that push the boundaries of form and content. This portfolio of activities provides more opportunities to view how a mind can be queered within a classroom to privilege the student experience over traditional academic texts. I will also be exploring the role of how queer culture exists as both a public and counterpublic within contemporary American society both inside and outside of the academy. By doing so, I hope to support the foundation of queer pedagogy through a sociological lens as well, rather than only a pedagogical one, to show the universality of the queer experience rather than just a topic for academic discourse.

By asking students to explore their minds and queer their writing process through Barry's activity, FYC instructors will become more critical thinkers and readers together as they guide their students to become more effective communicators. It is through expression and the human experience that we find connection to each other regardless of bias and separation. To find agency in the texts of ourselves through creative writing and queer composing alongside our fellow students and instructors, slowly but surely we expose our minds and become a bit more human. In queering the FYC classroom through creative writing, FYC no longer acts as a gatekeeper of the university but instead takes the gate off its hinges.

References

Alexander, J., & Rhodes, J. (2011). Queer: An impossible subject for composition. *JAC, 31*(1/2), 177-206. Retrieved from http://www.jstor.org/stable/20866990

Barry, L. (2008). *What it is*. Montreal: Drawn and Quarterly.

Butler, J. (1988). Performative acts and gender constitution: An essay in phenomenology and feminist theory. Theatre Journal, 40(4), 519-531. doi:10.2307/3207893

Conference on College Composition and Communication. (2014). *Students' rights to their own language.* Retrieved from cccc.ncte.org/library/NCTEFiles/Groups/CCCC/NewSRTOL.pdf

Harris, J. (2001). Re-writing the subject: Psychoanalytic approaches to creative writing and composition pedagogy. *College English, 64*(2), 175-204. doi:10.2307/1350116

Lunsford, A. (1979). Cognitive development and the basic writer. *College English, 41*(1), 38-46. doi:10.2307/376358

Murray, D. M. (2011). Teach writing as a process not product. In V. Villanueva and K. L. Arola (Eds.), *Cross-talk in comp theory* (pp. 3-6), Urbana, IL: NCTE.

Metacognition: Using Critical Reading Strategies to Promote Critical Thinking and Clinical Reasoning

Shirley Peganoff O'Brien & Camille Skubik-Peplaski
Eastern Kentucky University

Professional literacy requires effort in course design and implementation in content delivery. Reading disciplinary literature is a skill often underestimated in course construction. Educators employ metacognitive strategies to prepare students as critical thinkers through various content and activities. Through the use of effortful learning and focused feedback about critical reading techniques, students in this study were able to actively engage in preparation for professional reasoning in occupational therapy practice. Deliberate coaching in explicit critical reading processes did promote changes in critical reading strategies used in the course for student learning.

Introduction

Learning is not a spectator sport, especially in postsecondary educational venues. Faculty strive to promote metacognitive capabilities in learners as they share disciplinary knowledge through course content. Designing and creating the learning environment requires intentional planning to achieve desired course student learning outcomes. Faculty foster students' ability to actively use metacognitive processes to be fully engaged in the learning process through the use of various active learning techniques promoting effortful learning (Blythe, Sweet, & Carpenter, 2016; Winslow, Skubik-Peplaski, & Burkett, 2017). Learning how to apply content knowledge within various contexts takes the learner from basic understanding to broader application by engaging the student in effortful learning at a deeper level by explicitly outlining reading expectations.

Literature Review

Occupational therapy educators, similar to other disciplinary faculty, strive to promote metacognitive capabilities, fostering active control over the cognitive, self-regulatory processes needed for learning. Dinsmore, Alexander, and Loughlin (2008) defined self-regulation for learning as using strategies to plan, evaluate and revise to optimize learning. They further added from a neurobehavioral perspective the interaction between the person and the environment including emotional and contextual influences, which affect the experience of learning for the individual.

Reading is one of the primary avenues used in college courses for sharing foundational knowledge, yet is a skill often taken for granted (Wohl & Fine, 2017). Manarin, Carey, Rathburn and Ryland (2015) found that students often struggle to read well enough to comprehend disciplinary knowledge. The National Endowment for the Arts (2007) found that Americans are spending less time reading contributing to a decrease in reading comprehension and proficiency. Students known as iGen, may come to college without ever reading a book for pleasure (Twenge, 2017). A diminished ability to comprehend may affect a student's ability to critically think, reason and develop skill competency for future academic learning. Deliberately teaching professional literacy and engagement in the process is needed in disciplinary education at both undergraduate and graduate levels. Reading is a skill often assumed, yet takes effort and application of basic content. Effort in a learning situation, promotes deep learning that is more long-lasting and valuable to the student (Brown, Roediger & McDaniel, 2014; Winslow, Skubik-Peplaski, & Burkett, 2017). Intentionally structuring steps in the learning process with reading assignments helps the student to build confidence in their skill set, while promoting a stronger representation in the brain for retention and memory. When individuals learn with effort, they increase the survival of newly generated cells in the memory area of the hippocampus. As long as the learning experience is new, effortful, and successful, then these cells differentiate into neurons to form synapses and action potentials to create an advanced circuitry in the brain (Shors, 2014). Effortful learning can include self-regulation strategies, to enhance learning by interacting with the content, the environment, and then through planning, evaluating and revising. Zimmerman and Kitsantas (2014) describe the process of self-regulation as being able to attain and maintain cognition, emotion and behaviors to learn and assess your learning. Therefore, effortful learning with self-regulation techniques has initial and long-term benefits for the learner.

Brown, Roediger, and McDaniel (2014) share that when more effort is given in variable learning situations, learning is "stronger, more precise, and more enduring" (p. 68). The authors further espouse that when learning is slowed down and made more difficult—including steps that must be mastered—confidence is gained, and learning has a stronger representation in the brain. The more effort that is required to encode and consolidate during learning, the more the student reconstructs the components of the skill, making it pliable again. Learning then becomes clearer, reinforces meaning, and strengthens connections in the brain, while decreasing weaker competing routes. Massed practice, another often used technique, gives the illusion of mastery, but it uses short-term memory without having to reconstruct the learning from long-term memory. The effortful process of reconstructing the knowledge triggers reconsolidation and deeper learning (McGaugh, 2000). Thus, presentation of content and learning strategies for knowledge integration has many components for consideration.

Overview of Program Concepts

This project was initiated as the result of the authors' participation in a professional learning community (PLC) on critical reading. Critical reading is the focus of the institution's Quality Enhancement Project (QEP). The prior QEP focus was on critical and creative thinking, which provided a foundation to move toward how students read and build critical thinking abilities. Critical reading is defined as reading for purpose and success, which is espoused as a foundational skill for participation in society (Manarin, Carey, Rathburn, & Ryland, 2015). They further labelled two types of reading: transmission and transactional. Transmission reading contains basic meaning of content, often superficial while transactional reading is more engaging with advanced construction of meaning. Transmission reading often is seen as students use ineffective learning strategies, with minimal retention of information. Transactional reading requires effortful learning and self-regulation strategies that support the neurocognitive foundations for higher ordered thinking. Students often come into college courses using transmission reading skills: memorizing basic facts and relying on superficial knowledge. Students that are at-risk have lower academic performance and often present with less confidence in their abilities with a lower self-efficacy for learning (Komarraju & Nadler, 2013). Yet, to effectively critically think and reason, students must move to transactional levels bringing context into learning. This does not occur without focused pedagogical strategies, leading to metacognition and effortful learning.

As a result of our participation in the PLC, we decided to teach critical reading more transparently within one course. We established the following research questions:
1. Will students change reading practices following intentional reading instruction using metacognitive strategies in an Occupational Therapy course?
2. What are student perceptions about their growth in reading practices to promote effortful learning and in a professional discipline?

Method

Descriptive mixed methods were used in the construction of the Scholarship of Teaching and Learning (SoTL) research project. Institutional Review Board approval was obtained prior to initiating the study. Students in a 16 week semester entry-level professional research course in the occupational therapy program (n=31) were administered the Metacognitive Awareness of Reading Strategies Inventory (MARSI), as a pretest (week 3) and posttest (week 13) measure of reading abilities. The MARSI is a free tool, available on the web (Mokhtari & Reichard, 2002).

As a part of typical content delivery, students were assigned two research articles (quantitative and qualitative) to practice metacognitive strategies used in reading during weeks 4 and 6 respectively. The course instructor used role modelling techniques to demonstrate superficial (transactional) reading and deep reading strategies (transmission) to promote professional literacy about how to critically appraise quantitative and qualitative research articles. The course instructor role modeled habits and routines expected in disciplinary reading including awareness of self-regulation and activities to increase arousal and attention for effortful learning.

Discussions following the assigned readings focused on how to read and gain information categorizing reading as either transaction or transmission. Students were provided with practice opportunities, to reinforce retrieving, connecting and self-explaining (Lang, 2016) as best practices in learning. During Week 10, students provided qualitative feedback in response to a discussion board prompt about the use of targeted focus on the reading process in using occupational therapy research articles. This data was compiled and coded, using apriori critical reading definitions of transmission and transactional reading.

Results

Quantitative data yielded positive results about the changes in MARSI scores over the 10 weeks during a typical semester course. The MARSI provides an overall reading strategy score and subscale scores for Global Reading Strategies, Problem-Solving Strategies, and Support Reading Strategies. A paired-samples t-test (p=0.00) was conducted to compare changes in critical reading strategies pre and post metacognitive interventions for active learning. There were significant differences shown in all types of reading strategies (.000, .028 and .000). These results suggest that providing students with active learning opportunities and metacognitive strategies coupled with modeling critical reading techniques increases the development of effortful learning. Results are summarized in Table 1.

Qualitative data about how the students were using critical reading techniques in the course were invited and coded as transmission or transactional reading strategies. Both types of strategies were reported. Transmission reading comments were more logistical in nature with students recognizing the need to change their skill set.

"Graphs and charts really help me to understand difficult information."

"Re-read paragraphs and break them down sentence by sentence underlining and highlighting main concepts and bolded words."

Comments about the use of transactional reading strategies demonstrated a change in habits and routines in the reading process for course preparation.

"In this course I utilized more critical reading techniques than I have before. I am asking myself questions as I read to instill comprehension. I am writing clarification notes in the margins and I am summarizing what I am reading. Prior to this class my critical reading strategies were to prioritize my readings by subject headings and bolded words. It is important to be a better critical reader with research so that I can disseminate research effectively to be an evidence based practitioner."

"I try to make connections between the material I am reading and real-life situations. This helps me remember the information I am reading."

"When I am trying to study and retain the material for this course, I often quiz myself and ask questions about the content. I try to relate content to an experience or give a mnemonic device to content to help me remember the material as I read. I also outline and summarize the main points of the reading to try and get the bigger picture as another critical reading strategy."

Results suggest pedagogical emphasis is needed to teach

Table 1: Changes in MARSI Reading Score

Outcome	Pretest Mean	SD	Posttest Mean	SD	T	Df	sig
Global Reading Strategies	45.90	4.96	51.10	6.27	-5.41	30	.000
Problem-Solving Strategies	30.55	3.92	32.06	5.13	-2.30	30	.028
Support Reading Strategies	27.87	5.06	32.65	6.00	-5.05	30	.000

professional knowledge for evidenced based literacy. Once taught transparently, students respond and use the strategies for the advancement of their learning.

Discussion

The addition of teaching transparency in critical reading methods required small, powerful modifications in content delivery. The course instructor was deliberate, structured, with incremental modifications in course design resulting in significant changes in reading strategies used in the course. Students benefitted from critical reading techniques to facilitate deeper understanding of concepts to apply in practice transactional learning of disciplinary knowledge creating a more efficient skill capacity (Wohl & Fine, 2017). The deliberate teaching of reading strategies as well as the self-regulation techniques assisted the students to selectively use support reading strategies to improve comprehension of the material, thus building metacognition and reinforcing effortful learning.

Learning how to apply knowledge within various contexts takes the learner from understanding content as they consider themselves, and then others, coupling with knowledge of neuroscience and an understanding of adaptions needed when conditions may occur (Brown, Roediger, & McDaniel, 2014; Lang, 2016). The role of self-efficacy and self-regulation in promoting academic achievement is well documented (Komarraju & Nadler, 2013; Magi, Kikas, & Soodla, 2018; Yang, Potts, & Shanks, 2017). Placing learning into the context of the discipline takes effort, self-reflection and the creation of opportunities for application of basic content. Effortful learning requires self- regulation and focused attention. Thus, to gain mastery of disciplinary content, students must engage in reading tasks using multiple, research-based strategies (Brown, Roediger, & McDaniel, 2014, Wohl & Fine, 2017). Increasing reading comprehension facilitates understanding of discipline knowledge at a transactional level which improves skill competency and further builds a capacity for mastery. Fostering motivation through transparent teaching practices is paramount to the success in the college classroom. Faculty serving as facilitators of reading strategies can impact student learning. By the use of deliberate metacognitive strategies, faculty can assist students to role model, build confidence and promote techniques for managing and overcoming obstacles in the reading process.

Implications for Faculty Development

The key to success is to be deliberate in course design and delivery. Students arrive with varying sets of reading abilities. They need to learn how to read disciplinary materials differently for academic achievement. Faculty should role model the reading process expected when teaching disciplinary content including concepts of self-regulation. This helps forge an understanding of learning expectations, allows students to better appreciate the breadth and depth of disciplinary knowledge and socializes them into professional roles.

Another concept to explore is procrastination and how it fits into adaptive and maladaptive student habits and routines for learning with reading assignments. We, as educators tend to think hierarchically in building learning strategies for content success, much like the model presented in this article. Some students do work better under pressure versus out of a fear of failure or an emotional reaction to the given task of learning (Abramowski, 2018). Placing the learning outcome into a heterarchial learning context would be an interesting point to further the discussion about individual differences in promoting transactional reading.

References

Abramowski, A. (2018). Is procrastination all the "bad"? A qualitative study of academic procrastination and self-worth in postgraduate university students. *Journal of Prevention & Intervention in the Community, 46(2)*, 158-170.

Brown, P. C., Roediger, H. L. & McDaniel, M. A. (2014). *Make it stick: The science of successful learning.* Belknap Press of Harvard University Press: Cambridge, MA.

Blythe, H., Sweet, C., & Carpenter, R.G. (2016). *It works for me, metacognitively: Shared tips for effective teaching.* Stillwater, OK: New Forums Press, Inc.

Dinsmore, D. L., Alexander, P. A., & Loughlin, S. M. (2008). Focusing the conceptual lens on metacognition, self-regulation and self-regulated learning. *Educational Psychology Review, 20*, 391-409. http://dx.doi.org/10.10071s10648-008-9083-6

Komarraju, M. & Nadler, D. (2013). Self-efficacy and academic achievement: Why do implicit beliefs, goals, and effort regulation matter? *Learning and Individual Differences, 25*, 67-72.

Lang, J.M. (2016). *Small teaching: Everyday lessons from the science of learning.* San Francisco: Jossey-Bass

Magi, K., Kikas, E., & Soodla, P. (2018). Effortful control, task persistence, and reading skills. *Journal of Applied Developmental Psychology, 54*, 42-52.

Manarin, K., Carey, M.,, Rathburn, M. & Ryland, G. (2015). *Critical reading in higher education: academic goals and social engagement.* Bloomington, IN: Indiana University Press.

McGaugh, J.L. (2000). Memory -- a century of consolidation, *Science, 287,* 248-251.

Mokhtari, K., & Reichard, C. (2002). Assessing students' metacognitive awareness of reading strategies. *Journal of Educational Psychology, 94*(2), 249-259.

National Endowment for the Arts. (2007). To read or not to read: a question of national consequence. Washington, DC: National Endowment for the Arts.

Shors, T. J. (2014). The adult brain makes new neurons, and effortful learning keeps them alive. *Current Directions in Psychological Science, 23*(5), 311-318.

Twenge, J. M. (2017). *iGen: Why today's super-connected kids are growing up less rebellious, more tolerant, less happy–and completely unprepared for adulthood (and what this means for the rest of us).* New York, NY: Atria Books.

Winslow, M., Skubik-Peplaski, C., & Burkett, B. (2017). Transferring information from faculty development to classroom practice: A mixed-methods study. *Journal of Faculty Development, 31*(1), 35-40.

Wohl, H., & Fine, G. (2017). Reading rites: Teaching textwork in graduate education. *The American Sociologist, 48*(2), 215-232.

Yang, C., Potts, R., & Shanks, D.R. (2017). Metacognitive unawareness of the errorful generation benefit and its effects on self-regulated learning. *Journal of Experimental Psychology Learning, Memory and Cognition, 43*(7), 1073-1092.

Zimmerman, B. J. & Kitsantas, A. (2014). Comparing students' self-discipline and self-regulation measures and their prediction of academic achievement. *Contemporary Educational Psychology, 39,* 145-15.

Student Perception of Mindfulness Strategies' Impact on Student Learning

Jennifer Hight
Eastern Kentucky University

Recent trends in the literature indicate mindfulness can promote a classroom environment more conducive to student learning. By incorporating mindfulness strategies, student metacognitive abilities are fostered. This study explores the effects of mindfulness implementation in a college classroom to better understand student metacognition and perceptions of using mindfulness to promote learning.

Introduction

Recent trends in the literature indicate mindfulness practices can enhance student learning by fostering metacognitive abilities and promoting a classroom environment more conducive to teaching and learning.

Snapshot of the Emerging Adult Population

The majority of the student population currently entering college ages 18 to 29 are classified as emerging adults (Rathus, 2018; Rogers, 545). Emerging adults are unique in that they engage in extended role exploration, a luxury afforded populations in more "affluent nations" (Rathus, 2018, p. 257). Although they are no longer adolescent high school students; they are not quite ready to transition to the roles and responsibilities adulthood has traditionally brought with it (Rathus, 2018; Rogers, 2018). While emerging adulthood brings with it opportunities for identity exploration, and a sense of life's possibilities, it can include overwhelming changes, and uncertainty about the future which can lend itself to intense feelings of pressure and stress (Rathus, 2018, p. 258; Rogers, 2018, p. 546). Over half of young adults, 18 – 32 years old report increases in stress over the past five years (Rathus, 2018). The Smartphone generation has demonstrated a marked decline in social interactions with friends, are dating less, have less sex, and are in no rush to drive when compared with prior generations (Twenge, 2017a; Twenge, 2017b). In fact, this generation tends to view growing up as something to be deferred, and whom has termed the maturation process "adulting", as something to be avoided as long as possible (Twenge, 2017b, p. 45). While some may view the delayed transition of teens to young adults as inert, data from the Smartphone generation also reveals an increase in loneliness and decrease in sleep; giving rise to increased depression, suicidal ideation and suicide completion, the second leading cause of death for individuals ages 15 – 44 years old (Rathus, 2018; Twenge, 2017a). Therefore, it is important for college personnel and instructors to promote resilience in the college classroom to support learning and academic success (Rogers, 2018).

Literature Review

Mindfulness is defined as a mental state achieved through focusing one's awareness to the present moment, while calmly acknowledging and accepting one's feelings, thoughts, and bodily sensations (Google Dictionary, n.d.). Mindfulness strategies such as mindful breathing, meditation, relaxation activities, and movement provide an opportunity for students to unplug and connect to the present moment. Literature on the use of mindfulness has practical utility in structuring the classroom setting. Current evidence suggests incorporation of mindfulness strategies can promote academic success (Bray & Maykel, 2016).

Evidence suggests incorporation of mindfulness strategies in the classroom has the potential to enhance student learning and academic performance. Research suggests incorporation of mindfulness strategies in the classroom can support the transition of college students by reducing anxiety and stress; while promoting coping skills to support the emotional health of students (Crowley & Munk, 2017; Goretzki & Zysk, 2017). Pierdomenico, Kadziolka, and Miller's research *Mindfulness Correlates with Stress and Coping in University Students* deduce: "poor outcomes for distressed students may be reduced with mindfulness interventions"…, and "mindfulness training and practices are a reasonable method to combat stress by using healthy and productive coping strategies" (2017, p. 121-130).

In addition to the potential implications for psychological well-being, incorporation of mindfulness strategies in the classroom support student cognitive skills needed for academic success (Mrazek, Franklin, Philips, Baird, & Schooler, 2013 as cited by Goretzki & Zysk, 2017; Zeidan, Johnson, Diamond, David, & Goolkasian, 2010 as cited by Goretski & Zysk, 2017). Mindfulness can improve student executive functioning, concentration skills, attention, focus, mood, recall and memory (Crowley & Munk, 2017; Goretzki & Zysk, 2017; Zeidan et al., 2010 as cited by Goretzki & Zysk, 2017; Tang, Yinghua, Wang, Yaxin, Feng, & Lu, 2007 as cited by Goretzki & Zysk, 2017). A study by Ramsburg and Youmans reveals meditation, a component of mindfulness, "may positively influence decision making and motivation while completing a complex problem-solving task"; "may be an effective method for improving academic performance" (2013, p. 432). A study by Goretzki & Zysk found incorporation of mindfulness techniques demonstrated improved student retention and success, as well as life and study skills with students reporting: learning how to manage stress and relax, improved concentration, learning to stay more present, improved sleep, awareness of mental habits, and emotional regulation (2017).

Institutional or Program Context

This study explores potential implications of mindfulness strategies for student learning and metacognitive strategies in two disciplinary sections of a multi-section course (n=46). Not all students enrolled in the course sections comleted the varius phases of data coallection. The study incorporated a survey of metacognitive strategy use, and end of semester perspectives on the use of the mindfulness techniques. Data analysis yielded findings to promote classroom structure and considerations for learning. Exploration of this topic furthers faculty understanding of student populations in the promotion of teaching and learning.

Overview of Strategy, Approach, and Concept

The course instructor attended professional development on the use of mindfulness to promote learning. The author deliberately structured two sections of a multi-section course in occupational therapy intervention. The research question posed was: How does using mindfulness techniques in a college classroom enhance the self-awareness of students to promote metacognitive control of learning?

The research used a convenience sample of two class sections (one morning and one afternoon) of the same course over the duration of one semester taught by the author (Fall, 2017). Mindfulness activities were derived from two curriculums, Little Flower Yoga, and MindUp Curriculum which incorporate: breathing, connectedness, focused awareness, relaxation, and movement (Harper, 2016; Hawn Foundation, 2011).

Data Collection Related to Mindfulness and Metacognitive Strategies

The study incorporated a survey of metacognitive strategy use, and two end of semester surveys with perspectives on the use of the mindfulness techniques. The questionnaire explored topics related to student learning. The students provided information about personal study strategies, interpersonal communication to enhance understanding of course material, self-rewards, establishing goals and timelines. The electronic mindfulness survey explored various facets of student learning including: familiarity with mindfulness prior to taking the course, comfort with mindfulness strategies after taking the course, age appropriate populations, impact on student focus, impact on student stress, impact on student success, impact on arousal levels, impact on self-regulation, impact on learning environment, impact on social emotional learning, frequency of implementing mindfulness strategies before and after the course, and its impact on the student learner.

Analysis

Results of the Metacognitive Strategy Questionnaire

Metacognitive Strategy Questionnaire (MSQ). Response rate for completion of the MSQ was calculated after the first exam (76%) and after the second exam (67%). Students demonstrated a self-reported increase in the following metacognitive strategies: an increase in their ability to evaluate the quality of progress of work, rearrangement and organization of information to improve learning, set goals and timeline for studying the material, creating a plan to meet goals on time, arrangement of study environment, rewards self when reaching learning goal, asks a friend or classmate to help understand material, explain study strategies, and improved exam grade.

Results of the Electronic Mindfulness Survey

Students (n = 34) in both sections of the course were invited to complete an electronic Mindfulness survey at the end of the semester with 14 students in the morning section and 20 students in the afternoon session participating. Results of the survey revealed an increased comfort with mindfulness strategies after taking the course. Further results demonstrated the majority of all students who completed the survey (74%) reported mindfulness is applicable to all ages, improves student focus, decreases student stress, promotes student success, impacts arousal levels, promotes self-regulation, promotes a safe space for learning, promotes social emotional learning. Results related to transference of skills gained from engaging in mindfulness activities during class time were mixed: 50% of the students reported seldom implementing mindfulness strategies before the course and 38% reported seldom having plans to implement mindfulness strategies after the course. Almost half of the students surveyed reported frequent plans to incorporate mindfulness strategies in their area of practice.

Results of the Mindfulness Questionnaire

Results from both morning (n = 20) and afternoon (n = 20) sections of the course for a total of 40 students completing the mindfulness questionnaire at the end of the semester revealed perceived benefits and limitations of mindfulness, additional feedback, and application to student population. The morning session consisting of 20 participants identified benefits of mindfulness as calming, increasing focus, increases alertness/attention, decreases anxiety, decreases stress, promotes relaxation, and helps prepare for class. They identified limitations and additional feedback as taking away from class time, stressful or created anxiety, should be added into school routine for children, too difficult for children, and classroom was distracting. The students reported mindfulness is helpful to implement before a long assignment is due, as a tier one intervention, to increase focus and alertness, relaxation, tier 2 and 3, in-class to decrease negative behaviors, role fulfilment, and decreased anxiety. The afternoon session of the course with 20 students participating included benefits as decreasing stress, calming, increasing focus, increasing positive thoughts and increases alertness, coping strategy, and decreases heartrate. Students in the afternoon session reported mindfulness as being helpful before doing long assignments, as a heavy work break, transitions, calming activity, performance with children, as coping strategies, and increasing self-esteem.

Limitations and additional feedback included taking away from class time, stressful or created anxiety, too difficult for children, too individualized, and needs to be added into child's routine. So although students may perceive classroom insight as not needed, faculty do more than just deliver content. They foster a learning environment where students must take an active role in their learning. Even with the shift in metacognitive awareness scores and mindfulness increased comfort with mindfulness; taking away from class time was challenged. This suggests students enjoy learning strategies, but may not use the full bandwidth of skills learned when applied to their own learning. This finding was surprising, as emerging adults may find it easier to apply concepts to others rather than themselves.

Discussion and Considerations

Mindfulness Implications for Metacognition and Student Learning

Research suggests use of mindfulness strategies student cognitive skills needed for academic success (Bray & Maykel, 2016; Zeidan et al., 2010). Pierdomenico et al. (2017) research demonstrates the usefulness of mindfulness strategies in the classroom to support improved student outcomes. Goretzki and Zysk's research suggests: "learning mindfulness techniques to improve focus and concentration in a group setting has the potential to offer a cost and time effective model for staff and students. More broadly it demonstrates that mindfulness based interventions are applicable and appropriate to a tertiary setting and prove a unique model that can both support student well being and academic success." (p. 33).

Ancedotal data gathered suggests incorporation of mindfulness strategies in the classroom supports an environment conducive to learning, promoting calm and focus. Based on the Metacognitive Strategies questionnaire distributed after the first and second test, students further reported an increase in some Metacognitive strategies through the duration of the semester, improved exam grades throughout the semester, and an improved ability to explain study strategies. Thus, incorporation of mindfulness strategies served as a tool for assisting students in building their metacognitive skills through increased self-awareness of learning strategies. It provided an opportunity for students to self-monitor their learning strategies, and reflect on their learning.

The majority of students reported increased comfort with mindfulness strategies after the course, and felt mindfulness is applicable to all ages, improves student focus, decreases student stress, promotes student success, impacts arousal levels, promotes self-regulation, promotes a safe space for student learning, and promotes social emotional learning.

Emerging student themes related to mindfulness indicated it is calming, increases focus, increases alertness and attention, decreases anxiety, decreases heartrate, decreases stress, promotes relaxation, helps prepare for class, increases positive thoughts, coping strategy, increases self-esteem, is helpful prior to long assignments, and should be incorporated into child's routine. Limitations related to mindfulness strategies reported by students included: taking away from class time, stressful or created anxiety, should be added into school routine for children, too difficult for children, classroom was distracting, and too individualized. The data demonstrated graduate students thought mindfulness would be helpful for students, but not necessarily them. This suggests the skills did not transfer.

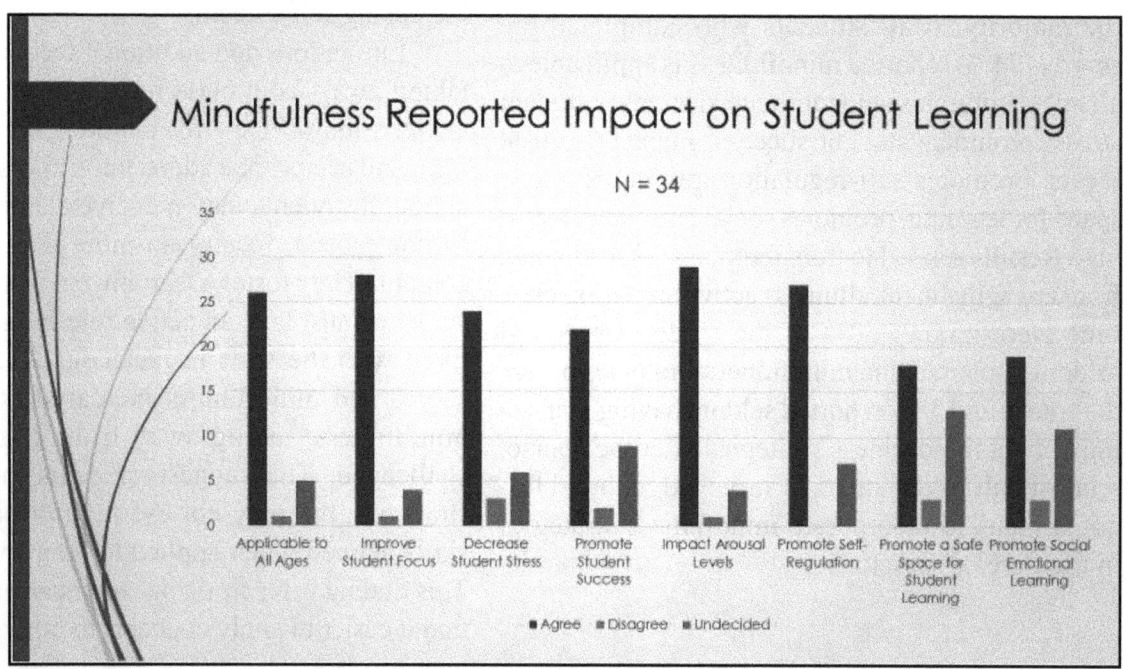

Figure 1

Implication for Fostering Student Learning

Implementation of mindfulness strategies can support student learning by fostering a calm, focused state of mind, and positive learning environment. Faculty can support student needs for refocusing through use of mindfulness teaching. Further, implementation of mindfulness can help enhance student self-monitoring, and self-awareness of strategies to improve metacognitive skills in learning. Thus, this study reinforced the clinical utility of mindfulness strategies in the classroom as a way of enhancing student metacognition.

Limitations & Implications for Further Research

This study did not have a control group. Students were graduate students in an entry level professional curriculum. Further research should incorporate students at earlier levels of undergraduate education to determine the impact of mindfulness strategies in relation to student learning. Further the time of day should be considered, as the needs of students and mindfulness strategies may need to vary between morning and afternoon classes. Future research should include following up with students enrolled in the classes which incorporated mindfulness strategies to determine if the students views on mindfulness changed, and with what frequency the student currently incorporates mindfulness strategies either individually or with student populations.

References

Bray, M., & Maykel, C. (2016). Mind-body health in the school environment. *International Journal of School & Educational Psychology*, *4*(1), 3-4. doi:10.1080/21683603.2016.1130528

Crowley, C., & Munk, D. (2017). An examination of the impact of a college level meditation course on college student well being. *College Student Journal*, *51*(1), 91-98.

Goretzki, M., & Zysk, A. A. (2017). Using mindfulness techniques to improve student wellbeing and academic performance for university students: A pilot study. *Journal of the Australian & New Zealand Student Services Association*, (49), 26-35.

Harper, J. (2016). *Yoga and mindfulness practices*. New York.

Hawn Foundation (2011). *MindUP Curriculum*. New York: NY: Scholastic.

Oxford Dictionary (n.d.) Definition of Metacognition and Mindfulness.

Pierdomenico, E. d., Kadziolka, M., & Miller, C. c. (2017). Mindfulness Correlates with Stress and Coping in University Students. *Canadian Journal of Higher Education*, *47*(2), 121-134.

Ramsburg, J. T., & Youmans, R. J. (2014). Meditation in the higher-education classroom: Meditation training improves student knowledge retention during lectures. *Mindfulness*, *5*(4), 431-441. doi:10.1007/s12671-013-0199-5

Rathus, S. (2018). HDEV5. Early Adulthood: Physical ad Cognitive Development.

Rogers, H. B. (2013). Mindfulness meditation for increasing resilience in college students. *Psychiatric Annals*, *43*(12), 545-548. doi:10.3928/00485713-20131206-06

Twenge, J (2017a). Has the smartphone destroyed a generation? *Atlantic*, *320*(2), 58-65.

Twenge, J. (2017b). iGen: *Why today's super-connected kids are growing up less rebellious, more tolerant, less happy – and completely unprepared for adulthood*. New York: NY: Atria Simon & Schuster.

Active Learning: Blending the Classroom in 3 Dimensions

Thad Crews
Western Kentucky University

Colleges and universities have seen considerable enrollment growth in online courses during the past decade. There is also growing interest in hybrid, blended, and flipped instruction to effectively incorporate technology into the teaching and learning process. This paper reports the results of a study of undergraduate student preferences for both face-to-face and online learning. An open response instrument was used to allow broad insights into students' responses without biasing or limiting the feedback. Study results provide practical insight for faculty interested in hybrid or blended course design. This paper also contributes a new perspective that extends classical instruction design learning theory and the role of technology with respect to active learning strategy in three dimensions. The results should be of interest to educators who wish to take a data-driven approach to using technology to improve teaching and learning.

Introduction

The history of higher education predates the printing press, with roots in medieval institutions established in the 11th century, which themselves evolved from earlier centers of learning (e.g., monastic schools, Madrasahs). The number of higher learning institutions grew and evolved because of the urbanization of European society (Colish, 1997; Grendler, 2004). Modern universities have progressed significantly from those of medieval times, and the curriculum has broadened considerably. One element that has been slow to change, however, is the frequency of classic face-to-face "sage on the stage" lectures which remain as the most common means of instruction.

Educational researchers have known for generations that these traditional lectures are not the best means to most effectively educate students (Dewey, 1913; Skinner, 1954). Different theories of education have been proposed, alternative pedagogical approaches developed, and various technologies introduced to increase options for improving the learning process (Prince & Felder, 2006; Rabbany, Takaffoli, & Zaiane, 2011).

The advancements of educational computer technologies in the past few decades has further increased the opportunities for change. Educational technology may refer to machines, computers, new processes, systems, and related approaches (Bates, 2005). Computers and networking technology are offering educators new and unique ways to connect with their students, inform, collaborate, and assess learning. The Internet has been particularly disruptive as it has allowed for education in other than a synchronous, co-located setting (Bates & Poole, 2003).

During the past decade, online education, in its various formats, has grown significantly in terms of student enrollment (Allen & Seaman, 2013; Clark & Mayer, 2007). Many traditional institutions have developed their capacity for online learning and non-traditional entities have emerged and thrive offering exclusively online programs of study. These developments have made learning opportunities available to people who may not have otherwise could take advantage of higher education. Students in underserved locations, adult learners, and even traditional-aged college students who live on college campuses are increasingly choosing to take courses in an online format (Bolkan, 2013).

Despite the growth in online enrollment and popularity of online courses, some student audiences, courses, and programs of study are not well-suited for this type of delivery system. There is growing interest in course-delivery methods that retain a significant element of traditional face-to-face content while augmenting the class with appropriate online elements. Hybrid teaching approaches including blended courses and flipped classes are actively being explored and adopted (Bonk & Graham, 2006; Keengwe, Onchawari, & Oigara. 2014).

The goal of these hybrid delivery models is to combine and leverage the beneficial features that are unique to ground-based with those that are unique to online courses. Like many new pedagogical approaches, instructors involved in hybrid-course design and delivery are still learning what does and doesn't work well for them. A growing body of anecdotal information is available on the web (Flipped Learning Network, 2014), but most early adopters are still largely left to their own experience to guide the process.

Although there is growing interest in flipped teaching, the approach is still relatively new and few educators have direct experience with it. One potential hindrance to more widespread adoption of a flipped teaching approach may be the simple heuristic commonly used to describe how such classes are designed. The popular explanation of whatever you used to assign as homework – do in class; and whatever you did in class – assign as homework may be suitable for some classes (e.g., a high-school math class), but may not map well to other areas.

As part of the overall effort to better understand and design hybrid courses, an exploratory study was undertaken. The goal of the study was to better understand what elements of face-to-face and online courses work well and should be considered for use in a hybrid class. A related goal is to determine which common elements of face-to-face and online courses are less effective. The objective is to identify the 'best of the best' characteristics from the perspective of the students, rather than the preferences of an individual professor. It is hoped that the findings will help guide future research in this area as well as provide educators with useful insights as they experiment with instructional design.

Method

The objective of this exploratory study is to identify the factors influencing students' positive experiences in both face-to-face and online classes. Student data was collected from a mix of 100-level, 300-level and 400-level university courses at a public institution. The university is well established, having offered traditional bachelor's for over a century and online degree programs since the late 1990s. The survey was designed to elicit the salient attitudes of students' experiences in face-to-face and online classes. Students also self-reported their gender (male-female) and generation (traditional student under age 25 or non-traditional student age 25 or over).

Consistent with the exploratory nature of the study, an open-ended questionnaire was used. Open-response surveys allow more insight to students' knowledge and permit a comprehensive collection of student responses without a-priori assumptions limiting the reporting (Nehm & Schonfeld, 2008). However, open response instruments also pose challenges. The first is that students may dislike writing answers, or not know how much to write for each response. To address the first challenge, the instrument was kept short, with the following open response questions:

Question 1: "Think back on the face-to-face (on-ground) classes you've taken. What were some of the characteristics of the best ones? What was it that made some stand out in your mind?"

Question 2: "Think back on the online classes you've taken. What were some of the characteristics of the best ones? What was it that made some stand out in your mind?"

Best of Face-to-Face Classes

Students' responses to the characteristics of their best face-to-face class experiences were revealing. The characteristic most frequently reported by students has having a positive impact on face-to-face learning experiences was "Interaction" which includes class discussions, group projects and other aspects of active learning. T-Test analyses were performed to compare "Interaction" to the other main categories, and the difference was statistically significant in each case ($p <= 0.03$). The positive reporting for "Instructor" was significantly below "Interaction" but was above the remaining main categories ($p <= 0.05$).

The positive characteristics of face-to-face classes were further sorted and analyzed per students' Gender and Age Group, with a significant difference found in the Gender results (Figure 1). It is noteworthy that females reported more positive elements for face-to-face classes than their male counterparts, even when adjusted for the larger percentage of female participants in the study (57%). Perhaps females are more tuned to the interactive possibilities of a face-to-face class. Perhaps males are more critical consumers of face-to-face classes. Regardless, in the highest reported category (Interaction), the female/male difference was statistically significant ($p <= 0.05$). So not only is Interaction the most important characteristic of a positive face-to-face learning experience, it is particularly important to female students. This finding is insightful and raises several interesting questions.

Best of Online Classes

The second question in the survey asked about positive characteristics of online courses, and again the results were informative. The characteristic most frequently reported by students for having a positive impact on online learning experiences was "Class Structure" which includes flexibility, schedule, organization, and clear expectations. T-Test analysis showed Class Structure to be statistically significant compared to each of the other main categories ($p <= 0.01$). The second most common response for positive impact in online classes was "Interaction", which was reported more frequently than any of the remaining categories ($p <= 0.01$).

The data suggest that the broad categories of Instructor, Material, and the Learning Management System (LMS) all lag Class Structure and Interaction as factors that positively impact online classes.

The positive online characteristics were sorted and analyzed according to students' Gender and Age Group, with a significant difference found in the Age Group results (Figure 2). Older non-traditional students were particularly impressed by good Class Structure and the difference on this issue between traditional and non-traditional was statistically significant ($p <= 0.01$). Perhaps this is due to non-traditional students having busier personal schedules, or perhaps they simply have come to appreciate the value of structure more than their younger counterparts.

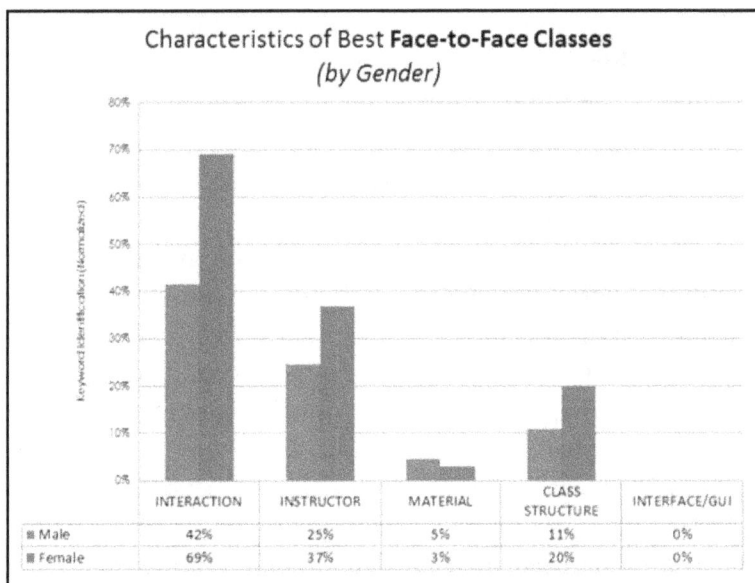

Figure 1: Face-To-Face Classes By Gender

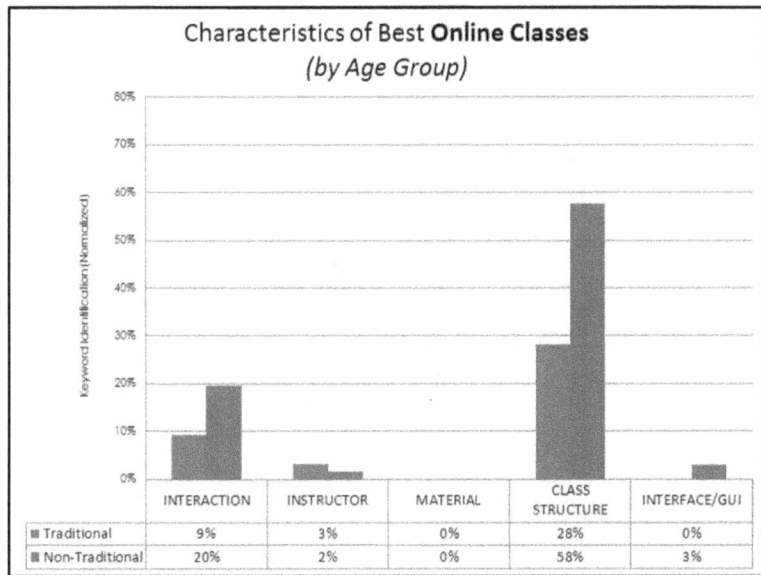

Figure 2: Generation Results for Characteristics of Best Online Classes

Discussion: Best of the Best

The results of this study provide useful insights that may be helpful for evaluating the many opinions and reported experiences associated with blending the classroom. The study used open response student data to better understand a blended classroom design based on the 'best of the best' approach of keeping what students report as the strongest characteristics of traditional face-to-face classes combined with what students report as best in their experiences with online classes.

The results are encouraging, offering insights by providing comparative analysis of student experiences comparing face-to-face and online classes. Furthermore, the findings are consistent with results of other research projects conducted using different instructional designs. For example, the findings show students value active learning and interaction during face-to-face meetings; including peer interaction through small groups and discussion. This is consistent with the pedagogical research which postulates that learning is an active process that is "situated" with both a social and cultural context (Vygotsky, 1978). The blended classroom provides great opportunities for students to bring outside of class reading and research into a very social interactive classroom discussion.

The findings also suggest that females are more positive than male students in their perception of the value of face-to-face classes. In particular, female respondents were significantly ($p <= 0.05$) more positive about the role of Interaction in face-to-face classes. Given the national trend of an increasing number of female students earning Bachelor's degrees (DiPrete & Buchmann, 2013), it would be interesting to extend the study to a program, department, or college level (rather than a multi-class level) to see if Interaction is a significant factor in major selection decisions by female students. This could be particularly insightful for programs seeking enrollment growth.

Active 3D Learning

The findings of the open response survey are consistent with longstanding best practice learning theory that emphasizes the importance of active learning in the classroom. Researchers of instructional design have long championed Active Learning strategies in the classroom (Bonwell & Eison, 1991; Paulson & Faust, 1998; Southerland & Bonwell, 1996). Active Learning theory suggests that the best learning occurs when both the student and the instructor are as actively engaged as possible. Figure 3 shows this active learning space in three dimensions.

The area labeled "Best Teachers (1966)" to reflect the TIME magazine May 6, 1966 cover story (Rosenblatt, 1966). The article discussed 10 faculty from different universities teaching in different departments (biology, history, psychology, literature, mathematics, chemistry, physics, etc.) The common thread for all these great teachers was their ability to have active, engaging classrooms rather than emphasizing one-directional lecture to passive students.

Modern instructional technologies allow for an increasing set of opportunities to present content in dynamic and engaging means. Figure 3 shows the learning space in three dimensions. Textbooks are perhaps the most static possible tool for presenting content, and it is no surprise that textbook publishers are looking for ways to move beyond textbooks to more interactive forms of content presentation. Likewise, there are departments, colleges, and even

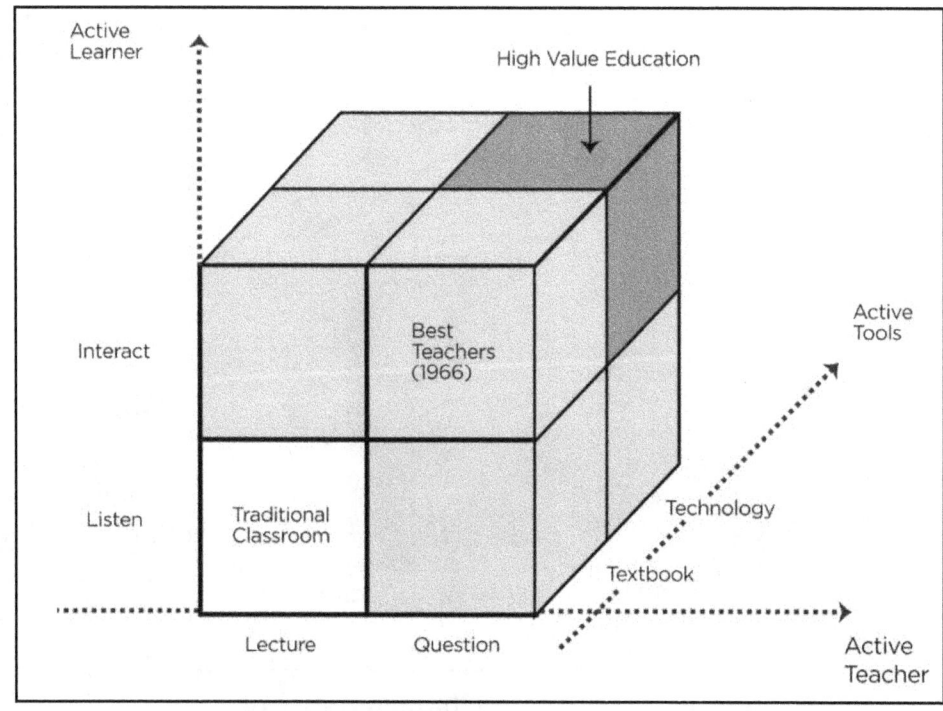

Figure 3. Active Learning in 3 Dimensions

institutions that are moving away from textbooks altogether (Associated Press, 2015).

The Active Learning 3D model intentionally does not specify the roles or specific strategies of the active teacher, the active student, or the active content tools because those details will be different from discipline to discipline and even from course to course within the same program. Regardless of implementation, the goal is clear: increasing activeness in all three dimensions will result in environments most favorable to learning.

Conclusion

The goal of teaching is learning. While each student is ultimately responsible for his or her own learning, the role of the faculty member is significant in terms of designing the environment in which student learning will occur.

Active learning is an old idea in instructional design research. However modern technology has reinvigorated these ideas by making it possible to record lectures for outside of class viewing and repurposing face-to-face class meetings for more interactive activities. Once again, technology allows old ideas to be revisited and improved.

The study presented in this paper shows that students reported class structure and interaction as the two class characteristics most responsible for a positive learning experience in an online class. The class characteristics most responsible for a positive learning experience in face-to-face classes were interaction and the instructor. The results are encouraging because these positive characteristics do not require dramatic administrative or technical change. Rather, meaningful small changes may result in a noticeably improved environment for learning.

References

Allen, E., & Seaman, J. (2013). Changing course: Ten years of tracking online education in the United States, Babson Survey Research Group. Retrieved from http://www.onlinelearningsurvey.com/reports/changingcourse.pdf

Associated Press. (2015, August 27). Maryland University to eliminate textbooks. *The Baltimore Sun*. Retrieved from http://www.baltimoresun.com/news/maryland/bs-md-umuc-no-textbooks-20150827-story.html

Bates, A., & Poole, G. (2003). *Effective teaching with technology in higher education*. San Francisco: Jossey-Bass/John Wiley.

Bates, A. (2005). *Technology, e-learning and distance education*. London: Routledge. doi:10.4324/9780203463772Sdf

Bolkan, J. (2013). Students taking online courses jumps 96 percent over 5 years, *Campus Technology*. Retrieved from https://campustechnology.com/articles/2013/06/24/report-students-taking-online-courses-jumps-96-percent-over-5-years.aspx

Bonk, C., & Graham, C. (2006). *The handbook of blended learning environments: Global perspectives, local design*. San Francisco: Jossey-Bass/Pfeiffer.

Bonwell, C., & Eison, J. (1991). Active learning: Creating excitement in the classroom. ASHE-ERIC Higher Education Report No. 1. Washington, D.C.

Clark, R., & Mayer, R. (2007). *eLearning and the science of instruction*. San Francisco: Pfeiffer.

Colish, M. (1997). *Medieval foundations of the western intellectual tradition, 400-1400*. New Haven: Yale Univ. Press.

Dewey, J. (1913). *The school in society*. Chicago, IL: University of Chicago Press.

DiPrete, T., & Buchmann, C. (2013). *The rise of women: The growing gender gap in education and what it means for american schools*. Russell Sage Foundation.

Flipped Learning Network (2014). Retrieved from http://flippedlearning.org (Retrieved 2014-03-06)

Grendler, P. (2004). The Universities of the renaissance and reformation. *Renaissance Quarterly*, 57.

Keengwe, J., Onchawari, G., & Oigara, J. (2014). *Promoting active learning through the flipped classroom model*. Hershey, PA: IGI Global. doi:10.4018/978-1-4666-4987-3

Nehm, R., & Schonfeld, I. (2008). Measuring knowledge of natural selection: a comparison of the CINS, and open-response instrument, and oral interview. *Journal of Research in Science Teaching, 45*(10), 1131-1160. doi:10.1002/tea.20251

Paulson, D., & Faust, J. (1998). Active learning in the college classroom. *Journal on Excellence in College Teaching, 9*(2), 3-24.

Prince, M., & Felder, R. (2006). Inductive teaching and learning methods: Definitions, comparisons, and research bases. *Journal of Engineering Education, 95*, 123-138.

Rabbany, R., Takaffoli, M., & Zaiane O. (2011). Analyzing participation of students in online courses using social network analysis techniques. *Proceedings of the Fourth International Conference on Educational Data Mining*, 21-30.

Rosenblatt, R. (1966). Teaching: To profess with a passion. *Time, 87*(18). Retrieved from http://content.time.com/time/covers/0,16641,19660506,00.html

Skinner, B.F. (1954). The science of learning and the art of teaching. *Harvard Educational Review, 24,* 86-97. doi:10.1037/11324-010

Sutherland, T., & Bonwell, C. (1996). *Using active learning in college classes: A range of options for faculty*. San Francisco, CA: Jossey-Bass.

Vygotsky, L. (1978). *Mind and society: The development of higher mental processes*. Cambridge, MA: Harvard University Press.

Podcasts for (Inter)active Teaching and Learning

Jason P. Johnston, Diane N. Loeffler, & Blake L. Jones
University of Kentucky

Much research highlights the use and the potential of podcasts in higher education. This paper examines the use of podcasts in the College of Social Work (COSW) at the University of Kentucky (UK) for student assignments, multiple means of course content, and program development. While examples of course content and program development are included, the paper focuses on the use of a student-created podcast assignment in an undergraduate social justice class. Literature and program context are briefly addressed before an overview of the assignment. The analysis uncovers some failures of the assignment, including lack of technical knowledge of the students, not utilizing student resources, and poorly managing the time needed to complete the project. The analysis also points to some successes, including a high level of assignment completion, positive student response, high grades, and collaborations between ethnically diverse students. The paper concludes with practical advice for teachers as well as an encouragement to continue research into the effectiveness of podcasts in higher education.

Introduction

This paper discusses "Using Podcasts for Student Assignments, Multiple Means of Course Content, and Program Development," a presentation on May 18th, 2018 at the Pedagogicon conference on the campus of Eastern Kentucky University. While the presentation covered a wide use of podcasts in the College of Social Work at University of Kentucky, this paper will focus primarily on how Diane Loeffler used a podcasting assignment to engage students in an undergraduate social justice class.

Literature Review

The use of podcasts in higher education has been touted as a means for students to enjoy portability, variety, and specialized instruction. There are thousands of podcasts available to educators, and the use of podcasts in distance education has become prolific. Podcasts have also been used to bridge the "digital divide," especially in rural states like Kentucky (Smith, 2010; Hew, 2009).

Despite the practice of and the perceived promise of using podcasts to meaningfully engage students, research on their impact is sparse. Numerous studies report student attitudes towards the use of podcasts (see for example McGarr, 2009; Vovides, et. al., 2007; & Merhi, 2015) and student familiarity with podcasts (Cassidy, Colmenares, Jones, et al., 2014). Fewer studies have examined whether or not podcasts increase student learning. There have been attempts to develop a conceptual model of how and why students use podcasts (Merhi, 2015), and these efforts have enhanced understanding of the multi-faceted issues at play (i.e., access to and previous use of technology, social factors, and faculty support).

The literature reveals that students tend to enjoy the medium of podcasting and it enhances their conceptual understanding of the material (Vovides, et al., 2010; Blok & Godsk, 2009; Ocepek, et al., 2011). Students use podcasting for both academic and recreational pursuits (Cassidy, Colmernares, Jones, et al., 2014). Podcasts can be linked to specific content in a way that students find enjoyable and entertaining, and flexibility has been noted by students to be a main benefit of using podcasts. However, traditional lectures are still seen by students to be relevant and helpful (McGarr, 2009).

When evaluating student use of technologies such as podcasts, it is important to examine the concept of student motivation. Several authors have found that the use of podcasts is linked to student motivation, and that students benefit from the way in which podcasts can be tailored to individual learning outcomes (Vovides, et al., 2010; Abdous, et. al., 2012; Abt & Barry, 2007). It is important, researchers note, that podcasts used in class are meaningfully connected to the content.(Ocepek, et. al., 2011; Obannon, et. al., 2011). Additionally, Hew (2009) found that students enjoy podcasts that are 15 minutes or less, and that other forms of information (i.e., PowerPoint slides, video lecture, etc.) should be presented along with the podcasts in order to augment the information presented to students.

While the literature is consistent in its review of student satisfaction with using podcasts, it is more mixed in terms of outcomes (Lakhal, Hager, & Pascot, 2007). Studies have shown that the link between satisfaction with this mode of delivery and actual increase in student learning is tenuous; experimental studies differ in their results related to podcasting and the enhancement of student outcomes (Abt & Barry, 2007; Merhi, 2015). Educators are cautioned to not simply use podcasts as a new and innovative way to engage students, but to be explicit in why they are using this pedagogical tool.

Program Context

The College of Social Work (COSW) at the University of Kentucky (UK) offers bachelors, masters, and PhD programs. UK has a mission to serve the Commonwealth of Kentucky. Most of the students in our program would call Kentucky home. In the last decade around 85% of our graduates have claimed Kentucky residency.[1] With the COSW main campus in Lexington plus a satellite campus in Hazard, the college tends to serve students in eastern Kentucky. Our Masters program is delivered with a combination of online and face to face courses while our undergraduate and PhD classes are almost entirely face to face. Beyond the COSW degrees, we offer some of our classes to a wider audience on the Lexington campus.

In our college, we implement podcasting in three different ways. First, as one of many ways of delivering course content. So, instead of simply presenting new material with a lecture, PowerPoint, and reading homework, an instructor could include listening to a podcast on the subject matter instead. This supports one of the main tenets of universal design for learning (UDL) which is to have multiple means of content representation (Rose, et al., 2006). This is also consistent with research that shows a need for podcasts to be utilized in conjunction with more traditional modalities such as lectures, reading, discussion, etc. (Hew, 2009). Second, we created a podcast as means of outreach and program development. In August of 2017, Jones and Johnston started a podcast series called "Social Work Conversations" that focuses on the research, teaching, and practice of professionals connected with the College of Social Work. As of this writing the podcast has had over 10,000 listens. These podcasts not only serve the wider community, with listeners from all over the world, but are now being used as content in our own classes. Finally, podcasts are used in our college as student assignments, where the students themselves are charged with the task of synthesizing material into a script and working in groups to record and produce their own podcasts. This student-centered aspect of podcasting is the remaining focus of this proceeding.

Overview of Approach

In January 2018, Loeffler and Johnston created a podcasting assignment for the Social Justice Foundations class (SW325) at the University of Kentucky. This face to face undergraduate class is open to all undergraduates and addresses social justice from a broad, introductory perspective. In Spring 2018 this ethnically diverse class of 65 students met together in a lecture and discussion format to learn about issues of power, oppression, privilege, and the rights of all people.

The purpose of adding this podcasting assignment was to engage the students in a new way using a current, popular media as a vehicle for knowledge synthesis. While written assignments have an important place in higher education, the idea surfaced that creating a new kind of non-written assignment might fulfill the same purpose but in a more compelling way. Loeffler and Johnston created an assignment that allowed the content of the podcasts created to be the focus of the assignment, de-emphasizing production value and time spent recording and editing. Similarly, grading criteria emphasized content over production value. The overall goal was to create a non-traditional way for students to present their own research, synthesis of information, and knowledge around power and op-

---

1. 2007-2017 Degrees Awarded Data retrieved from http://www.uky.edu/iraa/degrees-credentials-awarded

pression as it related to a specific problem relevant in the 21st century. These podcasts were shared between groups of students allowing for them to hear other student work and to engage in peer review and evaluation. Given concerns about technology, Johnston prepared resources that provided students with access to easy-to-use applications for smartphone and computer-based recording. Additionally, Johnston offered technical assistance to students by creating recorded step-by-step tutorials and videos which were placed in the online course shell.

Loeffler formed the assignment wording (see Appendix A) and rubric (see Appendix B), which centered on groups of 3-4 students who were to make a 7-10 minute podcast on a social justice topic of their choice. As part of the process, Loeffler created a "brainstorming worksheet" for the podcast topic idea to be approved by herself or the teaching assistant. Johnston prepared a Canvas instruction page with resources and tutorials for the students using their own equipment as well as the on-campus resources available to them. Johnston then visited the classroom at the launch of the assignment to explain the process in person and take any technical questions. At this time the school resources were also explained to the class through a video showing the podcasting recording room available to them in the student media depot. The students then had one week to submit their podcast topic for approval and then another month to record and upload the final podcast to the instructor's Dropbox folder.

Analysis

The podcasting assignment produced both successes and failures. The 65 students self-selected into podcast groups (N = 19), ranging from 2-5 students each. Groups were selected based upon mutual interest in social justice topics. Given the nature of the assignment, Loeffler and Johnston anticipated some "technology fails" but were surprised to find that some students were initially unable to record audio on their smartphones or to upload mp3 files. Surprisingly, not a single group reported using the University's podcast recording studio. All groups recorded on student laptops or smartphones. Additionally, Loeffler noted a time management failure on the part of some students. Approximately 25% of the groups were scrambling at the last minute to record and did not account for the time needed to complete the assignment, despite encouragement to start early. This is, however, not dissimilar from other group assignments wherein students often struggle to organize their time to meet and work as groups. An adjustment was made in response to student suggestions and discussion prior to the due date. Students who were not able to hand in a recorded podcast (due to technology failure or lack of time to coordinate the group members' schedules to record) were given the option to turn in a written transcript instead. In the end, 71% recorded a podcast while 29% submitted a written transcript. While the transcript was a different final product, it still achieved the goal of content engagement and synthesis and was graded using the same rubric.

There were also many successes, including the fact that 63 of 65 students completed a group podcast assignment. Even including the two scores of zero, the assignment grading average was 93%. Some student teams showed high engagement and produced excellent final products. From a teaching standpoint, this assignment allowed for multiple means of assessment and perhaps allowed students with developing writing skills to engage in an assignment that was not dependent on those skills. From a human standpoint, some kinds of collaborations may not have happened otherwise. In one case a young, African-American male student created a podcast with an older, white male student. The podcast started with a humorous, play-acted dialogue between them where the older student was claiming "not to see color." This set the stage for the rest of the podcast which engaged in a serious conversation regarding race and privilege. In this case, multiple levels of success were achieved. The podcasts (transcribed or recorded) allowed students' personalities and unique voices to shine, making the content interesting to their peers.

Though evaluation of the assignment was informal, student feedback was very positive. Students indicated they enjoyed the opportunity to submit a final product that was not a written paper and that they enjoyed the creative freedom the podcast project allowed. Students dissatisfied with the project were those who had problems within their own small group. Course evaluation data, which allows for open-ended student comments, captured several positive comments about the assignment.

Discussion

From many perspectives, the podcasting assignment was considered a success. It engaged the students, produced a high completion level, and gave the students an alternative from the typical written assignment. The assignment fostered higher order thinking in the students as they needed to synthesis material into a creative outlet. It also developed more technology capacity as they learned new techniques using their own equipment to recording and produce audio into podcasts.

Next time, we would hope to extend these podcasts outside the classroom as a type of real-world advocacy. Podcasting is a popular and growing media. A future idea would be to have the students join their voices into the public arena on their social issues of importance. One limitation this time was the lack of adequate free web hosting, which is necessary in order to release podcasts to iTunes and other such aggregators. A related change would be to use legal release forms so that the podcasts could be distributed freely beyond the classroom.

If instructors wished to use podcasts as assignments in their classes, our top advice would be the following: First, give adequate time for the students to complete the project since many of them will need time to learn the technology as well. Second, give clear assignment instructions with a complete grading rubric so that students will know how they are assessed. Third, and related, focus on the content and the learning experience, not on the sound quality of the podcast. Fourth, give generous instruction regarding any of the technology used and perhaps focus on technology that students are already familiar with like smartphones. Fifth, and finally, for increased engagement allow the students choose their own topics of interest within the parameters of the course learning objectives.

This pedagogical trial using podcasting as a student assignment was intended to be a practical exercise in course design and not a formal study. Further studies should be pursued to answer questions of effectiveness and student satisfaction in regards to podcasting as assignments. We hope that teachers will continue to try new techniques to engage students in important topics and that these student would in turn engage the world.

References

Abdous, M., Facer, B. R., & Yen, C. (2012). Academic effectiveness of podcasting: A comparative study of integrated versus supplemental use of podcasting in second language classes. *Computers & Education, 58*(1), 43-52.

Abt, G., & Barry, T. (2007). The quantitative effect of students using podcast in a first year undergraduate exercise physiology module. *Bioscience Education e-Journal, 10*(1), 1-9.

Blok, R., & Godsk, M. (2009, October). Podcasts in higher education: What students want, what they really need, and how this might be supported. In T. Bastiaens et al. (Eds.), *Proceedings of World Conference on E-Learning in Corporate, Government, Healthcare, and Higher Education, 2009* (pp. 117-128). Chesapeake, VA: AACE.

Cassidy, D., Colmernares, A., Jones, G., Manolovitz, L., Shen, L. & Viera, S. (2014). Higher education and emerging technologies: Shifting trends in student usage. *Journal of Academic Librarianship, 40*(2), 124-133. doi: 10.1016/j.acalib.2014.02.003

Hew, K. F. (2009). Use of audio podcast in K-12 and higher education: A review of research topics and methodologies. *Education Technology Research and Development, 57*(3), 333-357.

Lakhal, S., Hager, K. & Pascot, D. (2007) Evaluation of the effectiveness of podcasting in

teaching and learning. In G. Richards & S. Carliner, (Eds.), *Proceedings of World Conference on E-Learning in Corporate, Government, Healthcare, and Higher Education 2007* (pp. 6181-6188). Chesapeake, VA: AACE.

McGarr, O. (2009). A review of podcasting in higher education: Its influence on the traditional lecture. *Australasian Journal of Educational Technology, 25*(3), 309-321.

Merhi, M. I. (2015). Factors influencing higher education students to adopt podcast: An empirical study. *Computers & Education, 83*, 32-43.

O'Bannon, B. W., Lubke, J. K., Beard, J. L., & Britt, V. G. (2011). Using podcasts to replace lecture: Effects on student achievement. *Computers & Education, 57*(3), 1885-1892.

Ocepek, U., Bosnic, Z., Serbec, I., & Rugelj, J. (2013). Exploring the relation between learning style models and preferred multimedia types. *Computers & Education, 69*, 343-355.

Rose, D. H., Harbour, W. S., Johnston, C. S., Daley, S. G., & Abarbanell, L. (2006). Universal design for learning in postsecondary education: Reflections on principles and their application. *Journal of Postsecondary Education and Disability, 19*(2), 135-151.

Smith, A. (2010). Home broadband. *Pew Internet & American Life Project.* Retrieved from http://pewinternet.org/Reports/2010/Home-Broadband-2010.aspx

Vovides, Y., Sanchez-Alonso, S., Mitropoulou, V., & Nickmans, G. (2007). The use of e-learning course management systems to support learning strategies and to improve self-regulated learning. *Educational Research Review, 2*(1), 64-74.

Appendix A
Assignment Instructions

The following text was included in the assignment description in the class LMS (Canvas) shell:

You must clearly identify the topic and have it approved by your instructor/TA

Your podcast needs to provide information/education about the social issue and it needs to address what college students can do to affect change.

You will record your podcast (the UK Library has excellent support and equipment for you at *The Student Media Depot* – further information about how to record a podcast will be available via Canvas. Once recorded, you will upload your episode to the course Soundcloud account.

You will record a 7-10 minute podcast – further details in Canvas. You may choose to use media clips, but it is not necessary. Production quality will not be graded, though your podcast must be recorded such that it can be easily heard/is not difficult to understand. The expectation is not a professional podcast quality segment – so please consider your own time/expectations as you create the final project. Your production time should not exceed 5 hours total (recording, editing, splicing, etc.).

You are not merely reading an essay – your goal is to have a meaningful (if scripted) conversation that is educational, interesting, and that demonstrates critical thinking about the topic you've chosen.

Further podcast assignment information will be available in Canvas. GROUPS will be created within the first three to four weeks of class. Podcasts may be completed AT ANY TIME over the course of the semester (before the due date) – each group will upload their podcast for classmates to listen to and critique. Your final podcast grade is based on: 1) adhering to guidelines, 2) meaningful content, 3) timely submission, and 4) peer review.

DATES - groups formed FEB 9
TOPICS APPROVED - FEB 16
PODCAST DUE - APRIL 13
CRITIQUES OF CLASSMATES PODCASTS - APRIL 27

Appendix B
Assignment Grading Rubric

Criteria	Points Possible
The topic is educational, is well identified, and is connected clearly to social justice. This provides an appropriate background/context for the listener	2
The topic's tie to social justice is meaningful and demonstrates mastery of course content	3
The podcast is educational in nature — providing new information, asking questions, creating curiosity for the listener	2
What college students can do to affect change is identified, appropriate, and relates back to the topic	3
The recording (or transcript) is easy to follow, professional, respectful, and creative (this includes person first language, use of APA for references in written work, etc.	5

Designing an Online Course that Promotes Deeper Learning

Firm Faith Watson
Murray State University

How do online course practitioners design well-organized online courses that promote deeper learning, which equips students to transfer skills learned to novel situations? The answer to this question is significant because online course enrollments have been rising. This manuscript highlights the most relevant aspects of established course design frameworks: Wiggins and McTighe's backward course design; Dick, Carey, and Carey's instructional design model; Gagné, Briggs and Wager events of instruction; the Quality Matters rubric; and Bloom's taxonomy of learning; and relate them to practical strategies that online course practitioners may use right away to design deeper learning experiences in online courses.

Introduction

A recent trend in higher education is a shift toward facilitating deeper learning experiences (NMC Horizon Report, 2016), a general term for the 21st century knowledge and skills that students need to demonstrate to solve problems in their classroom and careers (Hewlett Foundation, 2013). What frameworks or strategies are useful for designing deeper learning experiences in online courses? The answer to this question is becoming increasingly important because online course enrollments have been rising steeply (Allen & Seaman, 2017).

The concept of deep learning is not new. As early as 1888, White noted: "Go below the surface; the richest treasures of thought are waiting for the skillful and diligent student" (White, 1923, p.127). Some researchers have distinguished between deep and surface approaches to learning (Marton & Säljö, 1976a; Marton & Säljö, 1976b; Biggs, 1987). Surface learning is associated with learning approaches such as rote memorization that gives a semblance of learning while deep learning approaches prompt students to seek for meaning, relations between certain concepts, and even satisfaction in completing certain objectives.

In recent years, only a few scholars such as Shearer, Greggand and Joo (2015); Czerkawski (2014); Garrison and Cleveland-Innes (2005); and Havard, Du, and Olinzock (2005) have investigated deeper learning in the context of online course design. According to Shearer, Gregg, and Joo, "there is a lot of investigation yet to do to continue to explore how to move students in fully online courses to deeper levels of understanding" (p. 132). For example, Garrison and Cleveland-Innes found that students' study approaches were strongly influenced by how the course was designed and taught. They concluded that "the reflective and collaborative properties of asynchronous, text-based online learning is well adapted to deep approaches to learning" (p. 145), and there is a strong need for research about teaching and learning approaches for online interaction. Over a decade later, Watson, Castano Bishop, and Ferdinand-James (2017) noted that there is paucity in the literature regarding how students "preferred instructional strategies inform existing theoretical and practical frameworks that could impact online learning performance" (p. 420).

According to Czerkawski (2014), "At the higher education level, using a well conceptualized instructional design is the best approach in applying deeper learning principles" (p. 37). This paper highlights the most practical aspects of established frameworks: Wiggins and McTighe's backward course design; Dick, Carey and Carey instructional design model; Gagné, Briggs and Wager events of instruction; the Quality Matters rubric; and Bloom's taxonomy of learning; and relate them to deeper learning approaches in the context of online learning.

Overview of Course Design Frameworks

Designing a Course Plan Using Backward Course Design

The backward course design framework, developed by Wiggins and McTighe (2005), prompts educators to: (1) identify the desired results of learning, (2) determine acceptable evidence, and (3) plan learning experiences and instruction successively. In the context of deeper learning, online course designers may ask these questions:

1. What skills should students acquire (objectives) that will result in deep learning?
2. What will I accept as evidence that students have acquired the skills (assessments) and will be able to apply them in their professional endeavors?
3. What learning experiences will help students to acquire the skills and apply them in real-life situations?

Perhaps the most seemingly illogical part of the backwards course design process is where the assessment is planned. The aforementioned questions show, however, that it is logical to consider what constitute acceptable performance (assessments) immediately after identifying the objectives. The answers to the questions help to ensure that the course objectives, assessments, and activities are aligned, which is necessary when designing deeper learning experiences.

Another established model that purports backward course design principles was designed by Dick, Carey, and Carey (2009). The components of the model are: identify instructional goals, conduct instructional analysis, analyze learners and contexts, write performance objectives, develop assessment instruments, develop instructional strategy, develop and select instructional materials, design and conduct formative evaluation of instruction, design and conduct summative evaluation, and revise instruction. In this model, assessment instruments are developed immediately after writing the objectives.

Considering assessment early in the instructional design process is also a key feature of the Quality Matters rubric which is becoming increasingly popular as a design standard for online courses. The sixth version of the rubric includes 8 general standards and 42 specific review standards. The general standards are: (1) Course Overview and Introduction, (2) Learning Objectives (Competencies), (3) Assessment and Measurement, (4) Instructional Materials, (5) Course Activities and Learner Interaction, (6) Course Technology, (7) Learner Support, and (8) Accessibility and Usability. The concept of alignment is crucial to applying the Quality Matters rubric, and standards two through six are critical components that must be aligned (Quality Matters, 2018).

Learning Context for Course Planning Worksheet. The aforementioned frameworks have clearly proposed that assessments be planned immediately after identifying the learning objectives and that key elements of the instructional design process be aligned. To this end, the course planning worksheet example (Appendix A) draws on these principles. The worksheet may serve as a guide for developing: learning objectives, assessments, instructional materials, and activities and interaction. The worksheet was originally designed to help faculty participating in an online course design institute to design their online courses.

Designing Online Modules

Perhaps what might be challenging is distinguishing between designing a course plan (using backward course design) and organizing a module, which involves a different sequencing of some of the components of the course plan (Appendix A). When organizing a module, online course designers may ask the following questions?

1. How will I prepare students to complete this module (Gain Attention)?
2. How will I let them know what's in it for them or the skills they will acquire (Learning Objectives)?
3. What materials, interaction and engagement are best to help them achieve the objectives (Learning Guidance)?
4. What opportunities will I give them to practice so that they will feel free to make mistakes as they try to master the objectives (Practice Activities)?
5. What will I accept as evidence that they have mastered the objectives (Assessments)?

The aforementioned questions were inspired by the work of Gagné, Briggs, and Wager (1992). They purported that there should be a lesson plan for assisting learners with their study efforts to achieve each learning objective. In cases where the lesson will be self-paced, a learner is typically presented with a module. They proposed nine events of instruction that support the internal processes of learning: (1) Gain attention, (2) Inform learner of the objectives, (3) Stimulate recall of perquisite learning, (4) Present the stimulus material, (5) Provide learning guidance, (6) Elicit the performance, (7) Provide feedback about performance correctness, (8) Assess the performance, and (9) Enhance retention and transfer. They explained that all the events need not be present in every lesson and that sometimes one or more of the events may be obvious to the learners.

Context for Module Organization Worksheet. Appendix B shows a module organization worksheet example that may be used as a guide to design deeper learning experiences. This worksheet was originally designed for participants in the aforementioned Online Course Design Institute. Figure 1 shows a collapsed version of the list of online modules. The names of the modules indicate the intended learning for the participants.

Figures 2, 3, and 4 show expanded versions of the list of components for modules 1, 2 and 3. The naming and organizing of the modules are consistent, which allow students to easily navigate through the course and engage in deep learning.

For each module, the learning guidance was presented in manageable chunks via two Canvas pages. In a study conducted with over 600 online students who answered the question: *What specific things would you like your online instructors do to help you learn successfully?* "Organize Course" was among the top 10 strategies. One student noted: "…

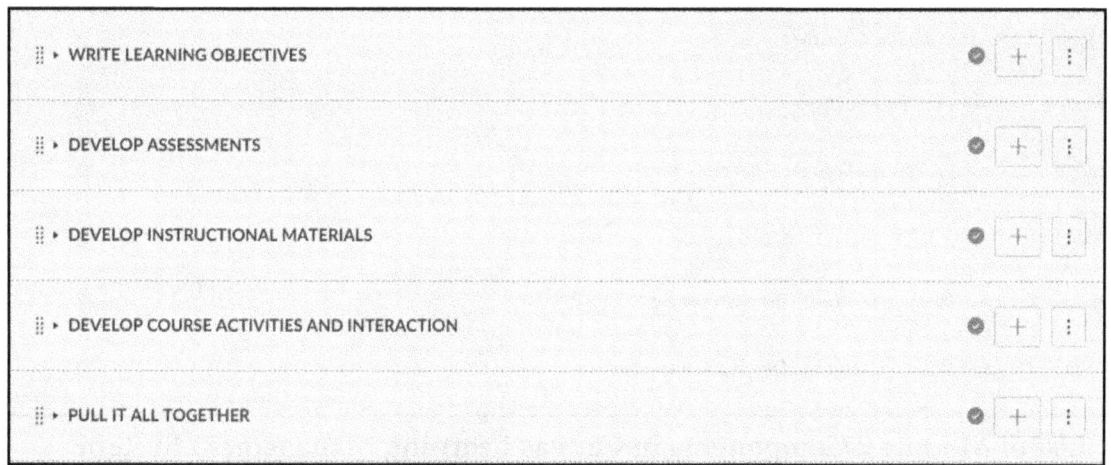

Figure 1. Excerpt of Modular List in Canvas Learning Management System

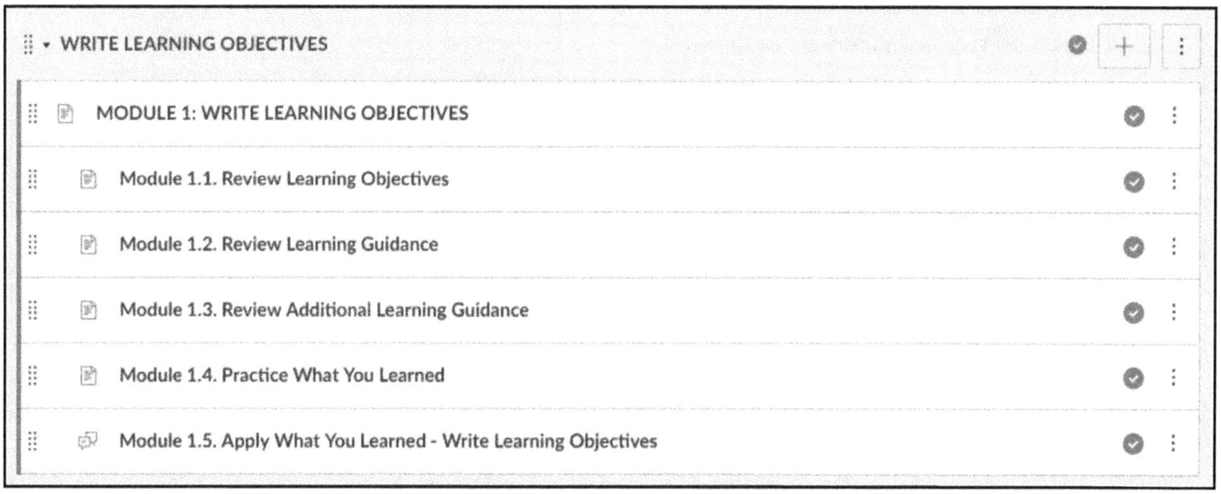

Figure 2. List of Module 1 Components in Canvas Learning Management System

it is highly beneficial to keep the courses structured, consistent, and concise" (Watson, Castano Bishop, & Ferdinand-James, 2017, p. 424).

There is, notably, a difference between the role of assessments while designing a course plan (Appendix A) and organizing a module (Appendix B). For the course plan, assessments are planned early (immediately after the learning objectives). For the module organization, assessments (particularly high stakes) are presented at the end of the module when students are expected to apply what they learned. In contrast, the low-stakes practice activities may be done earlier during the module.

On one hand, planning assessments early helps educators to determine what constitute acceptable performance of the objectives and design relevant course materials and learning experiences. On the other hand, when students are completing a module, they need to be informed of the objectives and provided with learning guidance and practice prior to being assessed.

Gagne, Briggs and Wager (1992) explained that the events of instruction may be used for teacher-led and learner-paced modular materials. A module usually "presents a learning objective, an activity guide, the materials to be viewed or read, practice exercises and a self-check test for the learner. In this case, the instructions or activity guide in the module is written for the student rather than for the teacher" (p. 28). They also noted that,

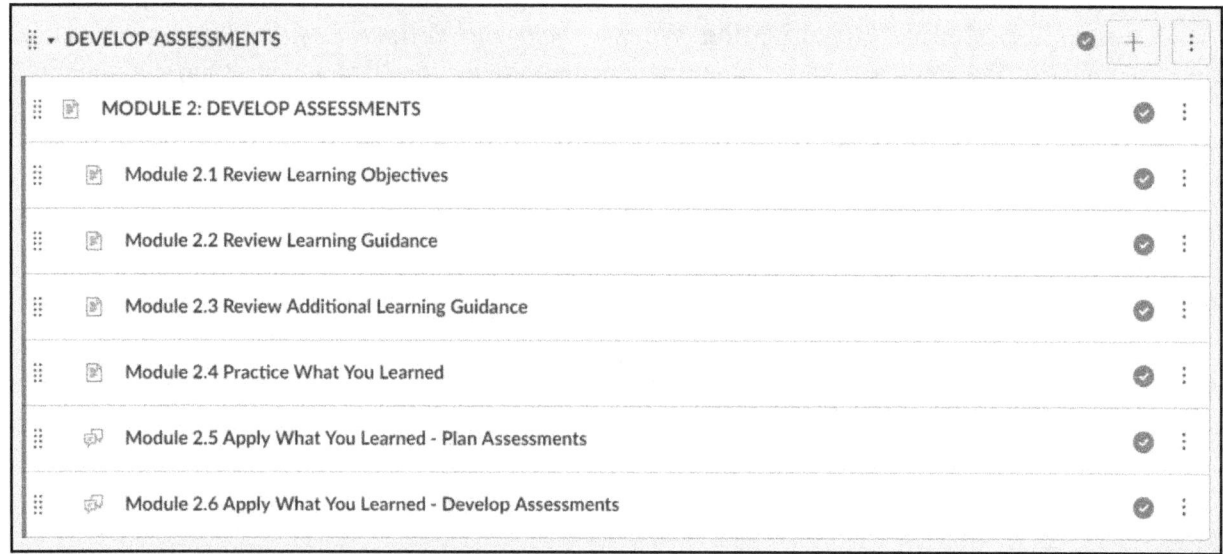

Figure 3. List of Module 2 Components in Canvas Learning Management System

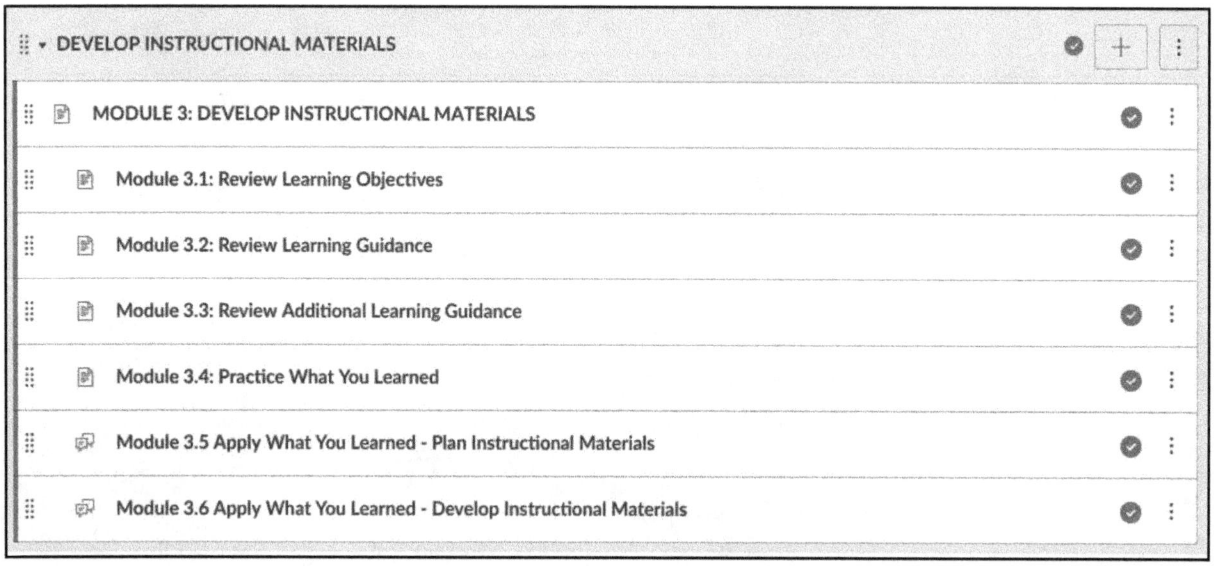

Figure 4. List of Module 3 Components in Canvas Learning Management System

in the model presented by Dick, Carey, and Carey (2009), the nine events of instruction would fall under stage 6 – Instructional Strategy.

Deeper learning cannot be expected if it is not planned for. Hence, it is important that the learning objectives, which provide the foundation for course alignment, be written in ways that challenge online students to demonstrate deep learning. One way to do this is by using verbs associated with different levels of Bloom, Engelhart, Furst, Hill, and Krathwohl (1956) taxonomy, popularly known as Bloom's taxonomy of learning, to identify the intended behavior of the objective. The revised version of the taxonomy has six levels of learning: remember, understand, apply, analyze, evaluate, and create (Krathwohl, 2002). The order of the levels suggests a progression from surface-level learning to deep-level learning. For example, verbs associate with the first level - *remember* - include: list, define, and label, while verbs associated with the last level - *create* - include construct, theorize, and predict.

Bloom's taxonomy also provides a schema for developing deeper learning questions and assessments in online courses. Such questions and assessments go beyond prompting students to recall factual information. While surface-level questions or assessments may be used, they should not be expected to result in deeper learning by themselves. Questions, for example, that require students to assess the arguments on which a premise is based are more likely to result in deeper learning.

Analysis (How does it work?)

The course planning worksheet (Appendix A) and module organization worksheet (Appendix B) provide examples for designing course blueprints and designing online modules that promote deeper learning respectively. These worksheets have some similar components, albeit in a different sequence.

In the context of the module organization worksheet, at the beginning of a module, one may **gain the learner's attention** via a deeper learning question (that requires more than mere recall of facts), metaphor, scenario or video. This way, students' interest in the objective is not assumed but purposefully planned.

The **objectives** should include verbs associated with higher levels of the Bloom's taxonomy that are aligned with the **learning guidance**, low-stakes **practice activities** and **assessments**. Therefore, if an objective requires students to analyze, they should be expected to do more than merely list or recall certain concepts during practice and assessments. In addition, the learning guidance section should provide resources that scaffold students' efforts toward analyzing certain concepts.

Designing two-week modules is also a means of promoting deep learning. For example, during Module 2 – Develop Assessment (Figure 3) - students planned assessment in one week and developed assessments the following week. A similar strategy was utilized by Shearer, Gregg, and Joo (2015). To facilitate deeper learning, they restructured a course from 12 lessons to six two-week modules. The students shared that "they enjoyed the two-week segments as it allowed them more time to reflect on the readings and to participate in richer discussions" (p. 130). Further, in the study reported by Watson, Castano Bishop and Ferdinand-James (2017), one student noted: "It is also very important that the assignments are spaced so there is enough time to get them done" (p. 425).

Throughout the course, the learning activities in each module should be linked to previous and subsequent modules, where applicable, and potential career opportunities. Importantly, students should be given opportunities to make the course activities relevant to their goals. This is congruent with another student's request in the reported study by Watson, Castano Bishop and Ferdinand-James (2017): "…allow us to pursue readings and assignments that match our long-term career interests" (p. 425).

Discussion and Consideration

This manuscript provides insights for applying established instructional design framework using deeper learning lens. Deeper learning in online courses does not occur without purposeful planning. This notion is supported by various researchers such as Entwistle (1982) who noted that the probability of deeper learning experiences increases when relevance, intrinsic motivation and interest are present in the learning environment. In contrast, assessments that encourage rote memorization and lack of concern for students' learning challenges increase the likelihood of surface learning. While effective teaching and assessment conditions do not automatically guarantee deep approaches, they help to make favorable learning conditions.

Good questions either from instructors or students can also achieve the aims of deeper learning. Yopp (1988) saw questioning as the beginning of thinking and noted that questions help students to be motivated, focused, and better able to estimate how well they are mastering the objectives. In this manuscript, Bloom's taxonomy of learning is presented as a tool for generating objectives, questions and assessments at deeper levels. For example, verbs associated with deeper levels of the taxonomy (apply, analyze, evaluate and create) are ideal for generating deeper learning objectives, assessments, questions, and supporting learning activities. This idea is in line with Yopp's conclusion that, "Asking higher-level questions by the students comprises a significant encouragement for deep learning processing" (p.1172).

The worksheets (Appendices A and B), images, and examples provided in this manuscript are just a tip of the iceberg needed to design deeper learning experiences online. Additional scholarly activities are needed to explore creative ways of designing online courses that promote deeper learning. Future research could investigate not only the design of deeper learning experiences but also the actual facilitation of such experiences. Key concepts such as instructor care and online presence for deeper learning should also be explored. Importantly, online students' perception of their deeper learning experiences should be investigated.

References

Allen, I. E., & Seaman, J. (2017). Digital learning compass: Distance education enrollment report. Babson Survey Research Group, e-Literate, and WCET. Retrieved from https://onlinelearningsurvey.com/reports/digtiallearningcompassenrollment2017.pdf

Biggs, J. (1987). *Student approaches to Learning and Studying*. Melbourne: Australian Council for Educational Research. Available at https://files.eric.ed.gov/fulltext/ED308201.pdf

Bloom, B., Engelhardt, M. D., Furst, E. J., Hill, W. H., & Krathwohl, D. R. (1956). *Taxonomy of educational objectives*, New York: David McKay Company.

Czerkawski, B. C. (2014). Designing deeper learning experiences for online instruction. *Journal of Interactive Online Learning*, 13(2), 29-40.

Dick, W., Carey, L., & Carey, J. (2009). *The systematic design of instruction* (7th ed.). Upper Saddle River, NJ: Pearson Education.

Entwistle, N.J., & Ramsden, P. (1982). *Understanding student learning*. Social Science Research Council, London. Retrieved from https://files.eric.ed.gov/fulltext/ED244959.pdf

Gagné, R. M., Briggs, L. J., & Wager, W. W. (1992). *Principles of instructional design* (4th ed.). Forth Worth, TX: Harcourt Brace Jovanovich College Publishers.

Garrison, D. R., & Cleveland-Innes, M. (2005). Facilitating cognitive presence in online learning : Interaction is not enough. *American Journal of Distance Education*, 19(3), 133-148.

Havard, B., Du, J., & Olinzock, A. (2005). Deep learning: The knowledge, methods, and cognition process in instructor-led online discussion. *The Quarterly Review of Distance Education*, 6(2), 125-135.

Krathwohl, D. (2002). A revision of Bloom's taxonomy: An overview, *Theory into Practice*, 41(4), 212 - 218. Retrieved from https://www.depauw.edu/files/resources/krathwohl.pdf

Marton, F. and Säljö, R. (1976a). On qualitative differences in learning. 1. Outcome and process. *British Journal of Educational Psychology*, 46, 4–11.

Marton, F. and Säljö, R. (1976b). On qualitative differences in learning: 11. Outcome as a function of the learner's conception of the task. *British Journal of Educational Psychology*, 46, 115-27.

NMC. (2016). Horizon report: Higher Education edition. Available at: http://cdn.nmc.org/media/2016-nmc-horizon-report-he-EN.pdf

Quality Matters. (2018). Quality Matters rubric standards. Retrieved from https://www.qualitymatters.org/qa-resources/rubric-standards/higher-ed-rubric

Shearer, R., Gregg, A., & Joo, K. (2015). Deep learning in distance education: Are we achieving the goal? *American Journal of Distance Education*, 29(2), 126-134, DOI: 10.1080/08923647.2015.1023637

Watson, F. F., Castano Bishop, M., & Ferdinand-James, D. (2017). Instructional strategies to help online students learn: Feedback from online students. Tech Trends, 61(5), 420-427. Available at http://rdcu.be/uY0J

White, E.G. (1923). *Fundamentals of christian education*. Nashville, TN: Southern Publishing Association. Available at http://www.truthfortheendtime.com/SOPText/PDF/Fundamentals%20of%20Christian%20Education.pdf

Wiggins, G. P., & McTighe, J. (2005). *Understanding by design*. Alexandria, VA: Association for Supervision and Curriculum Development.

William and Flora Hewlett Foundation. (2013). Deeper learning defined. Retrieved from https://hewlett.org/library/deeper-learning-defined/

Yopp, R. (1988). Questioning and active comprehension. *Questioning Exchange*, 2, 231-238.

Appendix A
Course Planning Worksheet Example

COURSE-LEVEL OBJECTIVES	MODULE-LEVEL OBJECTIVES	ASSESSMENTS	INSTRUCTIONAL MATERIALS	ACTIVITIES & INTERACTION
1. Write measurable module and course objectives at different levels of chosen learning domain (cognitive, affective, psychomotor).	1. Given a list of learning objectives or components of learning objectives, distinguish between the different components of the learning objectives (e.g. ABCDs).	1. Write at least three learning objectives at different levels of your chosen learning domain.	1. Scenario-based introduction to gain the learners' attention and prepare them for the learning objectives	1. Review the descriptions of the components (ABCDs) of a learning objective.
	2. Given descriptions of the different domains of learning (cognitive, affective, and psychomotor), distinguish between the different domains.	2. Indicate the level of the learning domain for each of the three stated learning objectives.	2. Descriptions of the components (ABCDs) of a learning objective	2. Review examples of learning objectives.
	3. Given verbs associated with the different levels of the domains of learning (cognitive, affective and psychomotor), select appropriate verbs to write objectives (at different levels of your chosen domain).	3. Write a brief reflection about your experience writing course and module objectives for your online course.	3. Explanation of how Bloom's Taxonomy can help	3. Review descriptions of the domains of learning: cognitive, affective, and psychomotor.
	4. Write at least three course-level objectives at different levels of your chosen domain(s) of learning (cognitive, affective, psychomotor).	4. Use the principles covered in Module 1 to provide feedback to at least one course developer regarding his or her stated learning objectives (while assuming the role of a student).	4. A guide to writing learning objectives	4. Review Quality Matters Standard 2.
	5. Write three or more module-level objectives at different levels of your chosen domain(s) of learning. The module-level objectives should be aligned with the relevant course-level objective.		5. Examples of learning objectives	5. Complete drag and drop activity: Create a 4-part learning objective by dragging the best component (A, B, C, or D) to its appropriate slot in the box provided.
			6. Descriptions and verbs associated with the three domains of learning: cognitive, affective, and psychomotor	6. Review learning objectives and identify the component(s) that might be missing (multiple-choice activity).
			7. List of Bloom's revised verbs	7. Use the learning objectives generator to practice writing learning objectives. Write a response for each prompt, review each objective generated, and revise where necessary.
			8. Learning objectives worksheet example	
			9. Quality Matters Standard 2 Annotations	

COURSE-LEVEL OBJECTIVES	MODULE-LEVEL OBJECTIVES	ASSESSMENTS	INSTRUCTIONAL MATERIALS	ACTIVITIES & INTERACTION
	6. Write a brief reflection about your experience writing your online course and module objectives. 7. Evaluate a course developer's course objectives and module objectives by assuming the role of a student in the course developer's online course and providing feedback.		10. Bloom's taxonomy interactive overview 11. Learning objectives generator 12. Learn and play objectives activities Supplemental Resources: 1. Writing good learning outcomes 2. Bloom's taxonomy (interactive version)	8. Write at least three learning objectives using the learning objectives worksheet template. 9. Post at least three learning objectives (written at different levels of your chosen domain of learning) via the discussion forum for feedback from peers and instructor. 10. Assume the role of a student and provide feedback to a course developer regarding his or her learning objectives (via the discussion forum).
2. Develop formative and summative assessments that are aligned with the stated online course and module objectives.	1. 2. 3.			
3. Develop instructional materials that are aligned with the stated online course objectives, module objectives, and student assessments.	1. 2. 3.			

Appendix B
Module Organization Worksheet Example

Module 1: Write Learning Objectives

COMPONENTS OF MODULE	NAME OF MODULE COMPONENT	DETAILS OF MODULE COMPONENT
1. Gain Learners' Attention Gain learners' attention via a deeper learning question (that requires more than mere recall of facts), metaphor, scenario or video, which prepares them to complete the objectives.	**Module 1: Write Learning Objective**	An image of an instructor (Martha) looking very thoughtful is displayed in the center of the Canvas page and students are presented with the brief scenario below. **Scenario:** Martha has an online course to develop. She understands the purpose of the course, however, she is not quite sure how to tell her students what they will get from the course or each module in a way that maximizes their learning. **What should Martha consider first?** What content would I like to cover? What would I like my students to do? Note for course designer: 1. Learners will select one of the choices above. Regardles of the answer selected, they will be directed to the next Cavas page: Module 1.1. Review Learning Objectives. 2. The strategy of allowing learners to see the need to 'pull' relevant information or resources is used throughout this module. This strategy is in contrast to 'pushing' the information on the learners.
2. Inform Learners of the Learning Objectives Inform learners of the learning objectives that you plan to guide them to achieve in the module.	**Module 1.1. Review Learning Objectives**	An image of an instructor (Martha) looking very thoughtful is displayed in the center of the Canvas page and students are presented with: (1) the best answer to the question in the aforementioned scenario and (2) the module objectives (derived from the course planning worksheet). Martha needs to first consider the skills that she would like her students to be able to demonstrate by the end of the course. A good way to do so is to write learning objectives at the course level and at the module level. By the end of this module, you will be able to do the following: Given a list of learning objectives or components of learning objectives, distinguish between the different components of the learning objectives (ABCDs). 1. Given descriptions of the different domains of learning (cognitive, affective, and psychomotor), distinguish between the different domains. 2. Given verbs associated with the different levels of the domains of learning (cognitive, affective and psychomotor), select appropriate verbs to write objectives (at different levels of your chosen domain). 3. Write at least three course-level objectives at different levels of your chosen domain(s) of learning (cognitive, affective, psychomotor).

COMPONENTS OF MODULE	NAME OF MODULE COMPONENT	DETAILS OF MODULE COMPONENT
1. Provident Learning Guidance Clarify major concepts, skills theories etc. And point students to relevant resources. If you have extra learning materials (that students do not absolutely need to achieve the objectives), include them in a supplemental resources section, so that students will know what to focus on.	Module 1.2. Review Learning Guidance	4. Write at least three course-level objectives at different levels of your chosen domain(s) of learning (cognitive, affective, psychomotor). 5. Write three or more module-level objectives at different levels of your chosen domain(s) of learning. The module-level objectives should be aligned with the relevant course-level objective. 6. Write a brief reflection about your experience writing your online course and module objectives. 7. Evaluate a course developer's course objectives and module objectives by assuming the role of a student in the course developer's online course and providing feedback. **Why Write Learning Objectives?** Learning objectives indicate the skills your students will be able to do by the end of a particular course, module or unit. The term learning objective is sometimes called learning outcomes. We will use both terms interchangeably in this institute. **Components of a learning objective:** **A - Audience**: Who - "The student will be able to..." **B - Behavior**: What learners are expected to be able to do **C - Condition**: The circumstances under which the skills should be performed **D - Degree**: The criteria or degree of acceptable performance When indicating the *behavior*, use clear verbs. The most popular domain of learning is the cognitive domain, which is often referred to as Bloom's taxonomy. There are, however, two other domains (see below) that may be relevant to your course. **Note**: You do not need to indicate the **audience** (i.e. the student will be able to...) at the beginning of every objective. You may consider using one introductory sentence (e.g., By the end of this module, you will be able to...) followed by the other components for each objective. **What would you like to review?** How Bloom's Taxonomy Can Help Three Domains of Learning (CAP) A Clear Guide for Writing Objectives Examples of Learning Objectives

COMPONENTS OF MODULE	NAME OF MODULE COMPONENT	DETAILS OF MODULE COMPONENT
3. Provident Learning Guidance (Cont'd)	Module 1.3. Review Additional Learning Guidance	*[Pyramid diagram of Bloom's Taxonomy, from bottom to top: Remember, Understand, Apply, Analyze, Evaluate, Create]* **How can Bloom's Taxonomy help?** An important aspect of writing learning objectives is **choosing the correct verbs** to indicate what exactly you would like your learners to do by the end of the course or module. The Bloom's Taxonomy of learning is a great tool to help you do so. The taxonomy was first developed in 1956 by Benjamin Bloom and a team of educational psychologists. In this institute, we will focus more on the revised taxonomy that was generated in the 1990s by one of Bloom's former students - Lorin Anderson - and a team of cognitive psychologists. A common mistake made by educators is to write learning objectives primarily at lower levels of the taxonomy (or vice versa) without reasonable grounds to do so. The resources below will help you to distinguish between the different levels of the Bloom's taxonomy. Your review will also help you to write more specific and measurable objectives at various levels of the taxonomy. **What would you like to do?** [Review Bloom's Taxonomy Interactive Overview] [Download Examples of Bloom's Revised Verbs]
4. Provide Opportunity to Practice These are usually low-stake activities that may be worth few or no points. They may include online quizzes, interactive activities, group work etc.	Module 1.4. Practice What You Learned	As you draft your course and module objectives, the activities below will help you to practice phrasing your objectives. You may find it helpful to refer to the learning objectives worksheet example, and practice writing course and module objectives with the learning objectives worksheet template. **What would you like to do?** [Fun Activity: Objectives Easy as ABCD] [Writing Learning Objectives - Practice] [Learning Objectives Worksheet Example] [Learning Objectives Worksheet Template] Think about the level of your course (100, 200, 300, etc...) as you practice writing your objectives. The domain level (e.g., remember or apply) at which you write your objectives will inform the level at which you write your assessments in the next module.

COMPONENTS OF MODULE	NAME OF MODULE COMPONENT	DETAILS OF MODULE COMPONENT
5. **Assess Learning** Provide high-stakes assessments. Students typically complete these independently. However, some projects may require collaboration.	Module 1.5. Apply What You Learned	**It's time to apply what you learned!** 1. Share your course and module learning objectives via this forum. • List at least three course objectives. Select one of your course objectives and list about three module objectives (written at different levels of your chosen domain of learning - e.g., Bloom's remember, apply and analyze). • Refer to the learning objectives worksheet example and Quality Matters Standard 2 for additional insights. • Use the learning objectives worksheet template to conveniently write and submit your objectives. 2. Post a brief reflection about your experience writing your objectives. 1. Assume the role of a student while reviewing a course developer's module and course objectives. Provide feedback (questions or recommendations for improvement) that will help you to picture how you would demonstrate mastery of the objectives. Provide your feedback by **(Insert date and time)**. 2. Add your course and module learning objectives to your **Course Planning Worksheet**. You'll be completing this worksheet as you progress through the institute, and it will help you lay out your ideas for designing your online course. Remember to update your worksheet if you revise your objectives.

Jigsaw Virtual Field Trips: Blending Teaching Strategies to Leverage Online Resources

April R. Hatcher & Sara B. Police
University of Kentucky

Virtual field trips (VFT) afford students a variety of experiences that are otherwise impractical due to cost and/or time impracticalities. Classically, VFTs explore the intricacies of popular destinations and/or activities, only digitally. The in-class assignment described herein challenges the stereotypical virtual field trip by proposing a variation to this activity, a virtual scavenger hunt, to encourage individual student ownership of their learning and an opportunity to contribute to the larger educational picture. This scavenger hunt approach is combined with the jigsaw method of information delivery. Jigsaw puzzles are comprised of small, individual pieces that create a larger, complete image when combined. The "jigsaw method" is an established teaching strategy that encourages students to pursue a particular piece of knowledge independently, and then integrate the piece within the broader 'picture'. We explored the utility of the jigsaw method within a virtual field trip framework. Herein authors describe the process used to entwine these two different approaches in a graduate level nutrition course. Benefits and challenges to this approach are discussed.

Introduction

Online higher education has experienced a boom of interest and expansion over the past decade. Emergence and optimization of the internet created virtual floodgates for information sharing, and the resulting rapid pace of change in regards to instructional strategies, academic courses and programs utilizing web-based interfaces makes assessment challenging and complicated. The Babson Survey Research Group examines the prevalence of online education by surveying chief academic officers at a large number of schools on a regular basis. According to 2014 estimates, about one-third of all students enrolled in college take one course online (with at least 80% of all content shared virtually) within a given year (Allen & Seaman, 2015).

The teacher/student interface for online learning employs many different formats (hybrid, fully online, blended, flipped, etc.) and occurs along a spectrum. At one end of the spectrum, there might be zero interactivity with an instructor; at the other, frequent interactions with peers and the instructor, perhaps through feedback within a discussion board format. Indeed, an overwhelming assortment of open online educational tools is currently available. McPherson and Bacow (2015) indicate the rapid speed of adoption within online instruction is a central reason underlying the lack of descriptive data about the extent of online strategies for different subject matters and varying segments of higher education. Considering this, it is important for educators to be selective when adopting online teaching strategies.

Field trips are usually a memorable, enjoyable learning experience for students (and many teachers), and research confirms their positive effect on student learning (Tuthill & Klemm, 2002). Logistical constraints such as time, safety, distance and expense are challenges to class field trips, and this is especially true for educators and students of higher and/or postsecondary education. According to Janet J. Woerner (1999), a virtual field trip (or VFT), is "a journey taken without actually making a trip to the site". In this sense, VFTs offer students limitless opportunities for their educational experiences.

The internet offers several forms of VFTs for a variety of teaching and learning environments and audiences (Tuthill & Klemm, 2002). Professionally produced multi-media VFTs combine various platforms (i.e. previously broadcast TV clips, video recordings, images) to broaden students' virtual experience and make connections with content, while teacher-made VFTs offer educators the opportunity to create a unique learning experience for a specific lecture, unit or course. Teacher-made VFTs are especially relevant for teachers looking to replace an actual field trip experience and/or when personalization with specific images and information is preferred. Web-authoring software (such as FieldtripZoom), digital cameras (or stock photos), relevant links and pertinent information are the only materials necessary for creating a unique, teacher-made VFT. Interactive virtual tours are readily available for over 50 locations in the Washington DC area, including famous landmarks such as the White House and the Smithsonian National Museum of Natural History. Furthermore, Google's 'World Wonders' project offers virtual tours of over 130 renowned global sites, such as The Sydney Opera House and Rievaulx Abbey (Google Cultural Institute website, 2013). VFTs designed as travel brochures are teaching tools for any geography, archaeology or history class, and are an excellent primer for an actual class trip to a specific location (Tuthill & Klemm, 2002).

Case studies utilizing virtual field stations to replicate actual field experience have reported positive outcomes. For example, Poland et al. (2003) examined the effectiveness of a virtual field station designed to replicate field work in the ecology and conservation of sea turtles. Specific assignments were designed to replicate actual fieldwork tasks with sea turtles. Their findings demonstrated that virtual field stations are an effective substitute for actual fieldwork in terms of developing student knowledge and understanding for examination and investigation (Poland et al., 2003).

All of these examples include instances where virtual reality replaces physical travel. However, the authors propose a modification to virtual field trips. Rather, a virtual scavenger hunt for information. The purpose of this class assignment was to explore the practicality and benefit of using VFTs within a graduate level basic science lecture. In particular, the authors aspired to augment teaching practice and student engagement.

Strategy
Design

The VFT assignment described herein employed the jigsaw method. Proposed by Aronson (1971), the jigsaw method "cuts" a block of knowledge into unique, interconnected pieces. The jigsaw method tasks students with independently mastering a specific "piece" of information that fits within a larger framework of knowledge. Teams of students are given responsibility for a specific piece, and then become "experts" on this content. In this way, new information is more manageable, and this is especially helpful when learning a new concept. According to Garcia et al. (2017), the jigsaw method is advantageous for several reasons, including increased student participation and interactions, as students gather and synthesize information rather than simply receiving the information from the instructor. This teaching strategy promotes deeper peer connections that cultivate a collegial learning environment.

Masters and doctoral students enrolled in a 3-credit graduate-level course (NS602; Integrated Nutritional Sciences II) participated in this class assignment. To encourage student participation, the VFT was built into an assignment worth credit toward the relevant exam. The class assignment described herein was tailored so that each team of students acquired their unique contribution (piece of the puzzle) via the virtual scavenger hunt. Per the assignment, either individual or paired students were given a student-learning outcome (SLO) directly related to lecture content, such as "Describe factors (dietary and non-dietary) that influence Fe (Iron) absorption ". Then, students were tasked to "travel" to pre-screened websites to locate relevant information to describe their SLO. Students prepared a 3-minute presentation of their choice (i.e. PowerPoint, handout, lecture) to reflect the information they found most pertinent to their SLO. Students were given one week to complete the VFT assignment and prepare their presentation.

Lessons Learned

The authors noted that students were engaged at various levels, as evidenced by a spectrum of class presentations. Some students instructed the class from handwritten notes while others created Powerpoint presentations to illustrate important concepts. While the various presentations did indeed add variety to the classroom hour, several lessons were learned regarding the overall success of our approach. One is that expectations for the presentation must be clarified, especially if this content will be tested formally. Rubrics set out specific criteria for various aspects of an assessment, and in doing so, clarify requirements and increase student success, especially when they are co-created by the students and instructor (Cockett & Jackson, 2018). Moving forward, future VFT assignments will include rubrics to establish standardization among students' presentations.

In addition, when implementing a new educational technique in the classroom, timing is critical. Some of the perceived student negativity toward this project was due to an exam on the content (plus additional unit material) within two days. This created feelings of anxiety as students were unsure what to focus on in their studies. The VFT assignment included specific learning objectives for each student to address in order to focus their study; however, too much variety among the quality of the student presentations lessened the usefulness of the listed SLOs. For this class assignment, the instructor followed each student presentation with an overview of testable concepts. Interestingly, others (Garcia et al., 2017) also report student inconsistency as a drawback to the jigsaw method. Ideally, including a rubric within future VFT assignments would encourage accountability on the part of each student to prepare and deliver a high quality presentation.

Moving forward, the authors plan to use IRB-approved surveys and specific measures to yield quantitative and qualitative data to more empirically describe the effectiveness of VFTs in nutrition graduate education. As described in Garcia et al., the final step of the jigsaw approach is for student learners to assess their peers. This step was not included in the class exercise described here, and would be a valuable reflective exercise to include in future iterations of this classroom technique. According to Zimmerman (1998), reflection is one of three key phases of self-regulated learning, with the preceding elements being forethought (planning for learning) and performance (monitoring learning). VFTs can promote self-regulated learning by requiring students to plan for class material, complete, and reflect on learning assignments in the course.

Discussion and Considerations

VFTs are valuable because they leverage open online resources by providing a focused and strategic framework for students within various teaching and learning settings. VFTs promote various pedagogical benefits focused on the learner, such as independence, engagement, and knowledge integration. As a diverse and multi-faceted teaching strategy, VFTs employ various forms and range from pre-packaged to teacher-made. Furthermore, VFTs are flexible, customizable and practical pedagogical tools for any academic level (i.e. secondary, postsecondary and professional levels).

The jigsaw approach is an accommodating teaching method applicable for essentially any learning environment, including online, hybrid, and traditional classroom. Reported benefits of the jigsaw method include increased active participation, increased self-esteem and focused attention spans (Garcia et al., 2017). The jigsaw method calls for students to integrate their "piece" of knowledge within the broader context, and to collaborate with peers in relevant shared activities and problem solving. In this way, each student uniquely contributes to the discussion. In effect, the jigsaw method augments teaching practice by requiring students to assimilate knowledge through collaborative learning.

The approach described herein utilized a modified jigsaw method within a VFT as an active learning exercise on the topic of nutritional anemia in a basic science graduate classroom. In the spirit of increased collaborative learning, the described class exercise could be enhanced by assigning virtual field trip assignments to small groups that work toward completion of a nutritional case study. In its current iteration, the jigsaw VFT assignment highlighted opportunities for improvements in future applications. Overall, the experience was beneficial and the authors are planning additional studies to investigate the utility of VFTs in graduate education.

References

Allen, I. E., & Jeff Seaman, J. (2015). Grade Level: Tracking Online Education in the United States. 2014. Survey of Online Learning. Babson Survey Research Group.

Cockett, A. & Jackson, C. (2018). The use of assessment rubrics to enhance feedback in higher education: an integrative literature review. *Nurse Education Today, 69*, 8-13. doi: 10.1016/j.nedt.2018.06.022.

Garcia, J A., Reguenes, R. (2017). Using the jigsaw method for meaningful learning to enhance learning and retention in an educational leadership graduate school course. *Global Journal Of Human-Social Science Research, 17*(5). Retrieved from https://socialscienceresearch.org/index.php/GJHSS/article/view/2249

Google Cultural Institute: World wonder project, 2013. Retrieved August 3, 2018 from https://www.google.com/culturalinstitute/about/wonders/

Lei, S. A. (2015). Revisiting virtual field trips: Perspectives of college science instructors. *Education, 135*(3), 323-327.

Kobayashi, K. (2017). Using flipped classroom and virtual field trips to engage students. *HortTechnology, 27*(4), 458-460.

Tuthill, Gail & Barbara Klemm, E. (2002). Virtual field trips: Alternatives to actual field trips. *International Journal of Instructional Media, 29*(4), 453-467.

Poland, R., Baggott la Velle, L. and Nichol, J. (2003). The virtual field station (VFS): Using a virtual reality environment for ecological fieldwork in A-Level biological studies-case study 3. *British Journal of Educational Technology, 34*(2), 215-231.

Veverka, J. (2015). Teaching outside the walls: Field trips help students understand the past and relate to the present as responsible citizens. *Journal of Adventist Education, 77*(2), 47-52.

Woerner, J. (1999). Virtual field trips in the earth science classroom. Retrieved from https://files.eric.ed.gov/fulltext/ED446901.pdf

Zimmerman, BJ. 1998. Academic studying and the development of personal skill: A self-regulatory perspective. *Educational Psychologist, 33*(2-3), 73-86.

New Technologies and How to Use Them: 3D and Makerspaces Demystified

Lesia Lennex & Justin Elswick
Morehead State University

New technologies bring learning opportunities to P-16 students. 3D technologies, in all forms, bring life to student productions. How do we support curriculum with these technologies? This proceedings discussion will bring perspectives and introduce projects in science, education, and design. Technical considerations for makerspaces and student production will be presented.

Introduction

In describing makerspaces and their possibilities, the method of a makerspace is a first consideration. This article presents two projects and three kinds of 3D printers. The first project, a summer camp for gifted children in grades three through nine, recently completed its tenth year. The second project, a hydropower analysis and design, was conducted with children in grades 6 through 12. Both projects incorporated engineering design software and 3D printers.

Project One involved scale modeling. Scale modeling is most often seen through hobbies such as dollhouse miniatures and train displays. Scale miniatures can be a gateway to learning engineering skills for 3D modeling. Children grades three through nine participated in a half-day, week-long summer camp for gifted and talented children designed to inspire their creativity and artistic expression The scale miniatures class was seventy-five minutes per day for four days and forty-five the fifth day By the last day, each child had created and decorated both a 1:24 scale dollhouse for a dollhouse and a 1:144 scale roombox, and printed a 3D creation of their design or choice This session shares construction of the 1:24 dollhouse, tips on working with gifted and talented children, and P-12 resources for 3D printing. In the second year, students created and printed two 3D projects. Creating objects for everyday use with engineering design is a prime example of goal fulfillment with STEM education and Next Generation Science Standards (NGSS).

Project Two involved an analysis of enclosed gravity-fed hydropower systems toward improvement of energy output. Hydroelectric power (aka hydropower) is utilized throughout the world. Gravity-fed hydroelectric power originating from glaciers is used heavily in South America, Europe, and British Columbia, Canada (Pelto, 2011). Hydropower is a form of renewable energy that uses the water stored in dams or flowing rivers to create electricity. The water is moved through a turbine that spins a generator that converts the mechanical energy into electrical energy. Hydropower utilizes the head (slope) and velocity of water. A good explanation of hydropower is available at https://www.youtube.com/7e26eb15-55cf-4d9f-86d9-a0bd6eeb3b96. Most of the hydropower generated in the United States is in the Pacific Northwest. About 13% of the renewable energy in the United States comes from hydropower. Hydropower has many advantages: It does not (1) pollute water or air, (2) adversely affect fish migration, (3) increase carbon dioxide emissions, nor (4) cause unnecessary removal of plants and animals.

There are several types of hydropower projects. Impoundments, such as Hoover Dam, are the most common, with 2,400 of the 80,000 existing dams producing power. Diversions, like Niagara Falls, are also known as *run-of-the-river* producers. Pump storage was the model for this project. Like the dam in Silvette, Austria that stores glacier water, this project utilized gravity-fed water to tank storage. Glacier run-off is of specific concern as it heavily influences at least half, or more, of all hydroelectric production in these nations. Water is a readily accessible resource for schools. It is also an incredibly dynamic source for exploration in biology, chemistry, physics, and engineering. Solving problems in delivering more energy from limited resources, such as glaciers, is a prime example of goal fulfillment with STEM education and Next Generation Science Standards (NGSS).

Literature Review

A makerspace may consist of numerous possibilities for student creativity. A makerspace exists to extend and explore a student's creativity. Makerspaces should provide numerous opportunities with differentiated materials from which students can design their own objects, textiles, wearable technologies, etc. (http://www.makerspaceforeducation.com/makerspace.html). For a makerspace with 3D printers, consider these resources: https://llennex.wixsite.com/kage2017/4.

Creating a makerspace utilizing 3D printers presents some usual and unique issues. The usual issues are choices in types of filament and resin. There are two types of medium: Acrilonytrile butadiene styrene (ABS) and Polylactic acid (PLA). ABS provides more strength to a print and is typically used for industrial applications. PLA is a naturally derived product and can be used for all uses aside from industrial applications (https://all3dp.com/pla-abs-3d-printer-filaments-compared). Chief among the unique issues, printers must be self-enclosed or operated in an enclosed, well-ventilated space. Aside from issues of older filament printers possibly giving rise to air-borne particulates, the filament printers produce copious amounts of heat. The extruders through which filament passes and becomes thinned for the print-layering process are potential serious burn sources. Print beds upon which the filament is layered for the object construction must be level and uninterrupted. If the system is open, it is possible for makerspace participants to be burned and/or cause print deviations that destroy the object formation. If a laser printer is used, one must consider the line-of-sight for all participants. Whereas filament is melted and cooled into additive lines for a filament printer, resin printers operate with lasers as fusing and drying agents. The lasers can cause permanent eye damage if observed on a consistent basis. Anecdotally, eye damage occurring as cotton wool spots (https://nei.nih.gov/faqs/retina-cotton-wool-spots) have been observed.

The primary 3D printers used in the projects were:

■ daVinci 1.0 Pro
- *Filament (ABS and PLA), proprietary and generic*
- *Spools of 600mg*
  Choice of infill (honeycomb or rectilinear) and percentage
- *Prints directly on print bed without excessive rafting*
- *Good detail*
- *Prints .stl and .obj files*
- *Inexpensive cost for printer ($300-$400) and proprietary filament ($23-$35)*
- *Minimal product support from company*
- *Extruder requires frequent maintenance*
- *No automatic shut-off if print is interrupted or goes awry. Possible occlusions from print clogs which require extensive maintenance*

■ Formlabs Form2
- *Resin (clear, tough, flexible, castable, dental in ABS and PLA options)*
- *Resin cartridges of 1000ml*
- *Cross-hatch infill*
- *Prints with support raft and choice support thickness*
- *Fine detail*
- *Prints .stl and .obj files*
- *Perfect prints each time*
- *Excellent product support*
- *Slightly higher cost for printer ($3300-$3500), necessary accessories (resin tray $50 for each separate resin used), and resin($150/cartridge)*

■ Stratasys Printer
- Filament (ABS and PLA), proprietary
- Choice of infill (default used in Project Two)
- Prints directly on print bed without excessive rafting
- Good detail
- Prints only .stl files
- Fantastic support (http://www.stratasys.com/resources/best-practices)

- Expensive initial cost ($15,000+) and large operating space (36 x 36 x 60inches)
- Print pads are required for each print ($20)

Project One's scale modelling generation is an excellent realization of engineering design. Not only were students educated about scale and design within the scales of 1:12, 1:24, 1:144, and 1:288, they were also required to employ knowledge of geometric patterns and shapes regarding construction techniques (https://llennex.wixsite.com/kage2017/kage18pageone). It is much more than a matter of reduction of design to appropriately accommodate change in scale. Supporting those designs with reinforced structural elements and/or creating new designs were key. Year two also incorporated a filament printer. Adjusting the infill on the filament printer is crucial. Whereas the resin printer required a minimum higher percentage of resin

Project Two's hydropower focus is an exemplar for the NGSS. Grubbs and Deck (2015) chronicled an experiment that responded to climate change by conserving energy. In this experiment, the turbine mechanism was altered, however, the materials used prevented precise measurement of energy conservation. Most experiments detailing turbine alteration involve wind machines and their production of energy.

Lent, Brown, and Hackett (1994), based on Bandura's (1977) theories of self-efficacy, produced a seminal work regarding social cognitive career theory. In it, three areas influence ultimate career choice: 1) development of basic academic and career interests, 2) determination of academic and career choices, 3) obtainment of academic and career success. Self-efficacy toward a career in engineering has been linked with undergraduate student interest and excitement (Mamaril, 2014).

Methodology

Project One: Children in grades 3-8 were enrolled in a gifted and talented summer camp. Children were given free choice of either two seventy-five minute classes or one three-hour class each day. The children enrolling to Art of Miniatures were involved in 3D design and production of scale models. The scale models consisted of one 1:24 laser-cut kit produced by Robin Betterley (https://www.robinbetterley.com/) for the National Association of Miniature Enthusiasts (https://miniatures.org/), one 1:144 hand-cut kit from Amy Rauch (https://miniatures.org/board, 2nd Vice-President), and models produced in all scales for 3D printing using a Formlabs2 resin printer. The daily schedule was as follows:

MONDAY
Agenda:
I. Introductions
II. Scale Models
III. Conversions and charts- hand out papers, show web site, discuss scale
IV. Introduce the Casita Bonita, its history, NAME
V. Begin construction of Casita – write name on base (side with Betterley's name)
   a. Dry fit
   b. In three sections, glue together each section
   c. Attach to base
   d. Allow to dry overnight
VI. Introduce 3D modeling
   a. Balloon demonstration
   b. Paper/pencils/markers for video on stairs—students create
VII. Go to GH 213
   a. Show short video introduction to TinkerCad
   b. Open Tinkercad – if time --

TUESDAY
I. Work in lab with TinkerCad
   a. Build tutorials 1-3
   b. Build tutorial dollhouse #4
II. Introduce Thingiverse
   a. Digital copyright (creative commons copyright)
   b. Allow students to explore thingiverse for "dollhouse"
   c. Save models to jump drive along with info
III. Introduce the Betsy Ross room
   a. Paint casita interior cream
   b. Paint casita windows white
   c. Construct and paint Betsy Ross room and fireplace white
      i. Measure exterior walls and floor for the paper cutouts

    d. Paint casita windows turquoise
    e. Paint casita ground khaki
IV. **if time, use the stain pens on Betsy Ross items as needed

WEDNESDAY
I. In GH 213 for construction of item for 3d print
    a. Display turbine models and discuss project briefly
    b. Display dollhouse chair model and painted chair (sprue/support and orientation)
    c. Students may search thingiverse or create own item
    d. Save student work to jump drive
II. If time, return to GH 209 and complete the interior of Betsy Ross

THURSDAY
I. Complete 3d Model for printing
    a. Save to thumb drive, transfer to Lesia computer
    b. Show video on Formlabs printer
II. Take class upstairs by 10am and 11:35am
    a. upload print (Class #2, save to drive and show printer)
III. Return to GH 209
    a. Show picture Amy's furniture
    b. Students design and build furniture for casita
IV. Painting and finishing
    a. Paint Casita exterior
    b. Assemble Betsy Ross interior
    c. Mix terra cotta with snowtex for exterior casita
V. Ask for speakers for class presentation (2 students – 1 from each class)
    a. Ask each to write down a word to represent their experience from class this week. Include to ppt for Friday.

FRIDAY

I. 45 minute class!
II. Glue on exterior finishing to Casita
III. Complete Casita and Betsy Ross
IV. Return 3D Models to students

Project Two: In this developing project, Middle and High School students used Solidworks (http://cad.about.com/od/CAD_CAM_Software/bb/Solidworks-2012-Review.htm) Educational Edition, to create propellers for water turbines. Students were given basic instructional tutorials within the program for SolidWorks. Students printed their original turbines using either a Stratasys Fortis 250mc (http://www.stratasys.com/3d-printers/design-series/fortus-250mc) or Mojo 3D (http://www.stratasys.com/3d-printers/idea-series/mojo) printer. After the experiment was conducted, we acquired two new 3D printers. One of the printers is a da Vinci 1.0 Pro by XYZprinting (http://www.xyzprinting.com/en-US/product/da-vinci-pro), and the other is a FormLabs Form 2 (https://formlabs.com/3d-printers/form-2). ABS filament is used in the Stratasys, Mojo 3D, and da Vinci, while the Form 2 is a resin-based printer. The design for hydropower was gravity-fed with electrical support from solar panels. Students tested their designs, measuring the energy output to determine which design was most productive. The design of turbine (Kaplan or propeller design) directly affected the amount of energy these systems could produce. This project allowed the design of the following propeller elements:
- Pitch
- Size
- Number of blades
- Shape
- Scoping of the blades

In addition to the main turbine experiment, students were also given pre- and post-experiment surveys gauging their self-professed knowledge of hydropower, their perceptions toward engineering and technology, and personal relevancy of a career in engineering.

Discussion

Students successfully created a 1:24 adobe dollhouse. The dollhouse would contain 1:288 scale furniture. Some students successfully scaled miniature furniture from Thingiverse to fit their dollhouse. Other students successfully created furniture from wooden "leftovers" and supplied scrap material for upholstery. The creation of both 3D-scaled and findings-based furnishings supported conceptual learning of three-dimensional space relationships and engineering design. Students further successfully created a 1:44 room box complete with furnishings and upholstery and a 3D design modification from Thingiverse. Based on anecdotal information, the class was highly successful in encouraging students toward pursuit of engineering and 3D production.

This pilot study reinforced the viability of teaching applied engineering and design software to middle school aged students. The design program used by students in this pilot could potentially support or repress engineering capacity among middle grades students. SolidWorks is an intense, CAD-based engineering design program. It is costly and extremely difficult to manipulate without extensive utilization. On average, we found that most students did not vary too much from the initial design parameters and tools presented to them. There are other programs which may affect the same improvement in self-efficacy in engineering. Subsequent pilot studies in 3D design used Tinkercad and Google SketchUp for initial design products. Finite controls, such as those present in SolidWorks, are necessary to achieve appropriate articulation of disparate parts within the overall turbine mechanism. Pilot studies are planned so that products such as Fusion360 may be evaluated for its use with school groups.

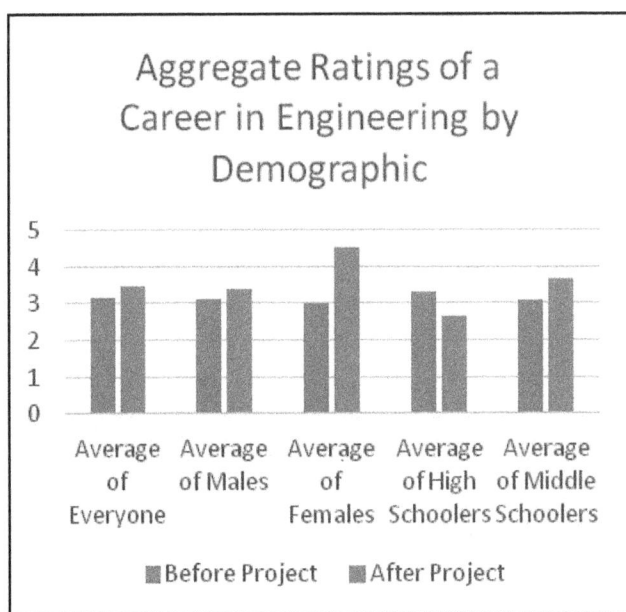

Graphic 1: Aggregate Ratings of a Career in Engineering by Demographic

Possible Uses in Higher Education

Makerspaces can be utilized for many kinds of activities that promote creativity. The materials for makerspace are quite varied. Many include legos, textiles, electrical activities, paper activities, as well as 3D design and manufacture. In higher education, having a creative space from which students can design and produce artifacts for use in their discipline demonstrates support of a student's curriculum application. By providing a space for students, universities have stated their continuing dedication to student independent inquiry and experiential learning.

References

Bandura, A. (1977). Self-efficacy: Toward a unifying theory of behavioral change. *Psychological Review, 84*(2), pp. 191-215.

Cordes, J., & Buck, R. (n.d.). Stratasys best practices. Retrieved from http://www.stratasys.com/resources/best-practices

Coppinger, J. (6 September 2018). What to know before you purchase SolidWorks, *Lifewire*. Retrieved from https://www.lifewire.com/before-you-purchase-solidworks-485240

Formlabs Form 2 (n.d.). Retrieved December 3, 2016 from https://formlabs.com/3d-printers/form-2/

Grubbs, M., & Deck, A. (October 2015). The water turbine: An integrative STEM education context, *Technology and Engineering Teacher*, pp 26-30.

Koslow, T. (17 April 2018). 2018 PLA Filament Guide- Explained, Compared & All Blends. Retrieved from https://all3dp.com/pla-abs-3d-printer-filaments-compared

Lennex, L. (2017), Kentucky Association for Gifted Education 2017 presentation page. Retrieved from https://llennex.wixsite.com/kage2017/kage18pageone

Lennex, L. (2018), Pedagogicon 2018 resources page. Retrieved from https://llennex.wixsite.com/kage2017/4

Lent, R., Brown, S., & Hackett, G. (1994). Toward a unifying social cognitive theory of career and academic interest, choice, and performance. *Journal of Vocational Behavior, 45*(1), pp. 79-122.

Mamaril, N. (2014). *Measuring undergraduate students' engineering self-efficacy: A scale validation study, doctoral dissertation*. Lexington, KY: University of Kentucky.

Matter Hackers (n.d). 3D filament guide. Retrieved from https://www.matterhackers.com/3d-printer-filament-compare

National Association of Miniature Enthusiasts (n.d.). Retrieved from https://miniatures.org/

National Eye Institute (n.d.). Retrieved from https://nei.nih.gov/faqs/retina-cotton-wool-spots

Pelto, M. (2011). Glaciers and hydropower. Retrieved from http://www.nichols.edu/departments/glacier/glacier%20runoff%20hydropower.htm

Robin Betterley's Miniatures. (2017). Retrieved from https://www.robinbetterley.com/

Rocket Science (2015, August 1). How hydroelectricity works? Retrieved from https://www.youtube.com/7e26eb15-55cf-4d9f-86d9-a0bd6ee-b3b96

Roffey, T. (2016). Makerspace for education. Retrieved from http://www.makerspaceforeducation.com/makerspace.html

SolidWorks (n.d). What to know before you purchase SolidWorks. Retrieved from http://cad.about.com/od/CAD_CAM_Software/bb/Solidworks-2012-Review.htm

Stratasys Fortis 250mc (n.d.). Idea series. Retrieved from http://www.stratasys.com/3d-printers/design-series/fortus-250mc

Stratasys Mojo (n.d.). Mojo magic at your desk. Retrieved from http://www.stratasys.com/3d-printers/idea-series/mojo

Thingiverse (n.d.). Featured collections. Retrieved from https://www.thingiverse.com/

Tinkercad (n.d.). From mind to design in minutes. Retrieved from https://www.tinkercad.com/

XYZprinting (n.d.). da Vinci 1.0 Pro. Retrieved from http://www.xyzprinting.com/en-US/product/da-vinci-pro

Adjusting Teaching Practices to Benefit Generation Z Learners

Gaby Bedetti
Eastern Kentucky University

Students are different today than they were even a few years ago. In many ways, they are more challenging to teach because they are uncomfortable with authority. A current practice that contributes to student-centered learning, especially deep learning, is to target students' learning styles. The author surveyed an upper-level literature class to determine the students' preferred learning styles. The guidelines emerging from her study suggest a course format that keeps communication brief, enables co-creation, and allows for one-on-one interaction. While these findings are consistent with current research about Generation Z learners (Cilliers, 2017; K. Mohr & E. Mohr, 2017; Seemiller & Grace, 2016; Sweet, Blythe, & Carpenter, 2018), the study found that the guidelines are not typically the basis of current practice in the English major. With the raised confidence and interpersonal skills resulting from such teaching practices, however, the degree recipient in any field will prove a more agile and collaborative professional.

Introduction

Given the 16% decline in humanities degrees in the last six years, if the liberal arts are to survive, instructors must find ways to make them more viable. Students are different today than they were even a few years ago. In many ways, Generation Z (also known as iGeneration, born after 1995) is more challenging to teach because—unlike their instructors—Gen Zers are uncomfortable with authority (Cilliers, 2017). Once teachers recognize how today's students are different, they can adjust to their learning styles. Recently instructors have succeeded in drawing students back to literature surveys, for example, by shifting course outcomes away from acquiring content and toward developing skills (Kalata, 2016). Modernizing course goals and practices may draw students back to the humanities. The purpose of my study was to identify practices that engage Generation Z and cultivate marketable critical thinking and communication skills. My findings propose a teaching style that keeps communication brief, enables co-creation, and allows for one-on-one interaction.

Institutional Context

This investigation examines today's literature classroom at a regional state university in central Kentucky. The resurgence of active learning in the 1990s would suggest that, thirty years later, instructors have transformed their teaching practices. Like Buchanan, however, I wonder whether the English Education majors in my upper-division courses are "encountering models of teaching in literature classes that undermine what they are learning in methods courses" (2016, p. 79). To collect opinions about teaching practices in literature courses, I surveyed students in a core course for the English major, ENG 353, to examine pedagogical approaches in 2017 in the context of the Modern Language Association's findings from faculty (Charon et al., 2009; Houston et al., 2001; Huber, 1992). My aim was to contribute a field report from the classroom that revealed how Gen Zers learn.

The need for and relevance of a study of English majors' learning styles stems from the "yawning gap [in pedagogy] between writing studies and literary studies" (Corrigan, 2017, p. 550) and the decline of English majors. As bachelor's degrees awarded nationally have increased by 34%, the English major has taken a precipitous downward turn (Laurence, 2017). From 2012 to 2017, English degrees fell 17%, though communication degrees increased 8% (American Academy, 2018a; Bureau, 2018). A more recent source claimed that "at many institutions the decline in humanities majors since 2010 is over 50% (Hayot, 2018).

Unfortunately, studies of upper-division literature courses as a unit are even fewer than studies of introductory courses, validating the belief that we are not concerned enough with how we teach literature to our majors (Buchanan, 2016). As with most universities, nearly 80% of my department's undergraduate course offerings fulfill the university's arts and humanities requirements, supporting other majors across the institution with courses in reading, writing, and research. Meanwhile, the English teacher shortage has reached a crisis point. For the English degree to survive, English teachers need to "to engage in experiments that will allow us to shift and adapt to new ecosystems" (Hayot, 2018). Our practices need to adjust to benefit Generation Zers' lives in the new economy.

Overview of Approach

A report prepared by the MLA's director of research based on the organization's 1990 study has provided the most comprehensive data available on the course format in the English major to date (Huber, 1992). First, Huber found that, on average, instructors devoted an equal amount of class time in upper-division literature courses to lecture and discussion. Second, she found that instructors who had received their highest degree within the ten years prior to the survey devoted more time to discussion than instructors who had received their highest degree more than ten years before the survey. The latter finding anticipated a shift away from lecture that has since become more firmly rooted—in theory, if not in practice. However, the 1990 MLA Survey concluded that "traditional... practices remain in place" (Huber, 1992, p. 51).

A few years later, two studies conducted at medium-sized regional state university whose participants were students in beginning and upper level English courses (Beishline & Holmes, 1997; Richardson, Kring, & Davis, 1997) yielded similar findings. Students clearly preferred lectures (albeit with an additional element such as voluntary participation, demonstrations, or student discussion groups) by contrast to professor-assisted class discussion. However, female students liked a more interactive approach to teaching, and students with the highest GPAs overwhelmingly preferred class discussion. These conclusions about students in all English courses appeared to reinforce the MLA's earlier finding of traditional course format.

My study sought to identify the preferred learning styles of Generation Z English majors. I posited that interactive learners absorb more than solitary learners do, and specifically, that participants who enjoy discussing their reading experience learn more than students who prefer listening to the instructor lecture.

To test the hypothesis, I designed the course to include a variety of brief in- and out-of-class solitary and interactive activities. Solitary activities included submitting a five-question online reading quiz and reviewing the correct answers, preparing a five-minute cultural context presentation, posting an open-ended response to the reading, composing a creative response, and listening to the instructor lecture. The interactive activities included replying to participants' responses to the reading and reading responses to one's own post, as well as replying to responses to the creative task, reading responses to one's own creative task, and discussing everyone's response to the reading assignment.

Analysis
Participants

The group studied was a cameo of national English major demographics. The twenty participants represented the varied concentrations at our comprehensive regional university, which requires a minimum ACT of 18 for full admission. The participants' year in college, as shown in Figure 1, indicates that most students were well along in their courses for the major, with the largest population being seniors, followed by juniors and sophomores. The largest percentage were seniors (40%) and had completed the other core upper-division literature courses. The group also mirrored the gender distribution of degrees in English since the late 1960s, as it was comprised of fourteen women (70%) and six men (30%). One student was African-American (5%), which is characteristic of the racial/ethnic distribution of degrees in English (American Academy, "Racial/ethnic," 2018). Finally, one student was nontraditional (5%), defined as over the age of 24.

Furthermore, Figure 1 regarding participants' major concentrations indicates that this group represented national trends. Given the upsurge of creative and technical writing, it is not surprising that 40% had a concentration in technical or creative writing rather than literature. Unfortunately, despite the shortage of English teachers (Teach, 2018), only 20% were majoring in English Teaching. In sum, the group studied closely represented the national distribution of English majors.

Procedures

To begin, I received the approval for my study from Institutional Review Board at Eastern Kentucky University. For my investigation of the learning styles of English majors, I selected a survey of British literature since the late 1700s. On the first day of class, after I reviewed the course syllabus and oriented the class, students received an Informed Consent Form, which described the study, stipulated that participation was voluntary, and assured their anonymity. Twenty students consented to participate.

My research methods were both quantitative

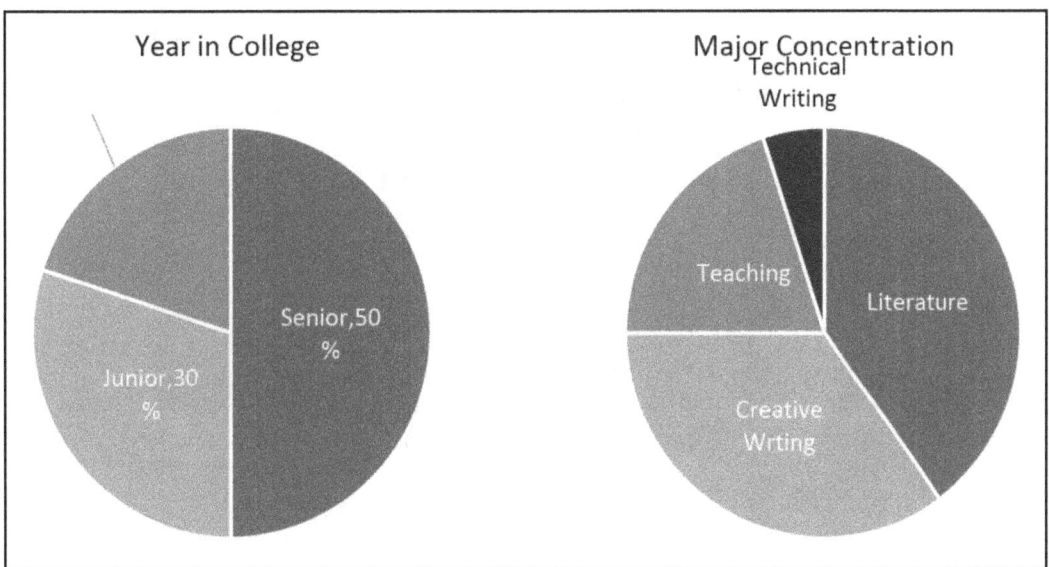

Figure 1. Participants' Demographic

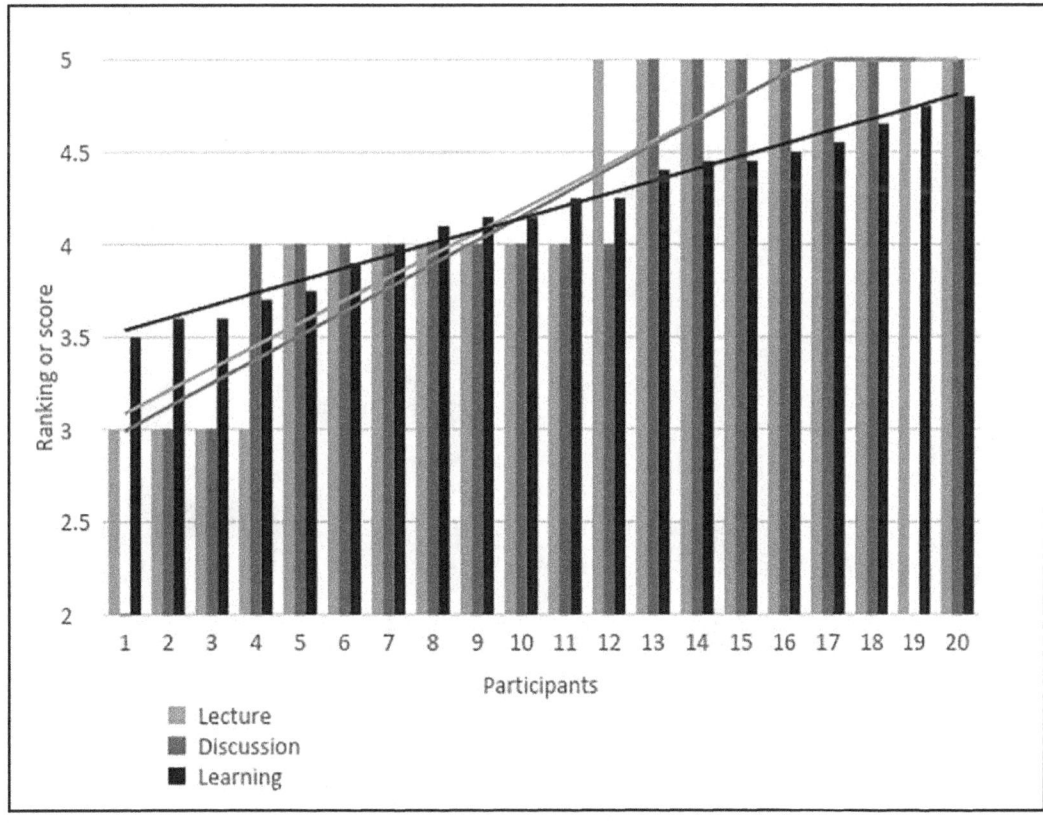

Figure 2. Contribution of Lecture and Discussion to Learning for Unit I

and qualitative. Within a week of completing the study of a literary period, participants completed an online questionnaire reflecting on the recent unit. The first six questions invited participants to rank activities on a Likert-like survey. The second six were questions invited students to comment on their learning styles and the various class activities, as well as to estimate the ratio of class time devoted to

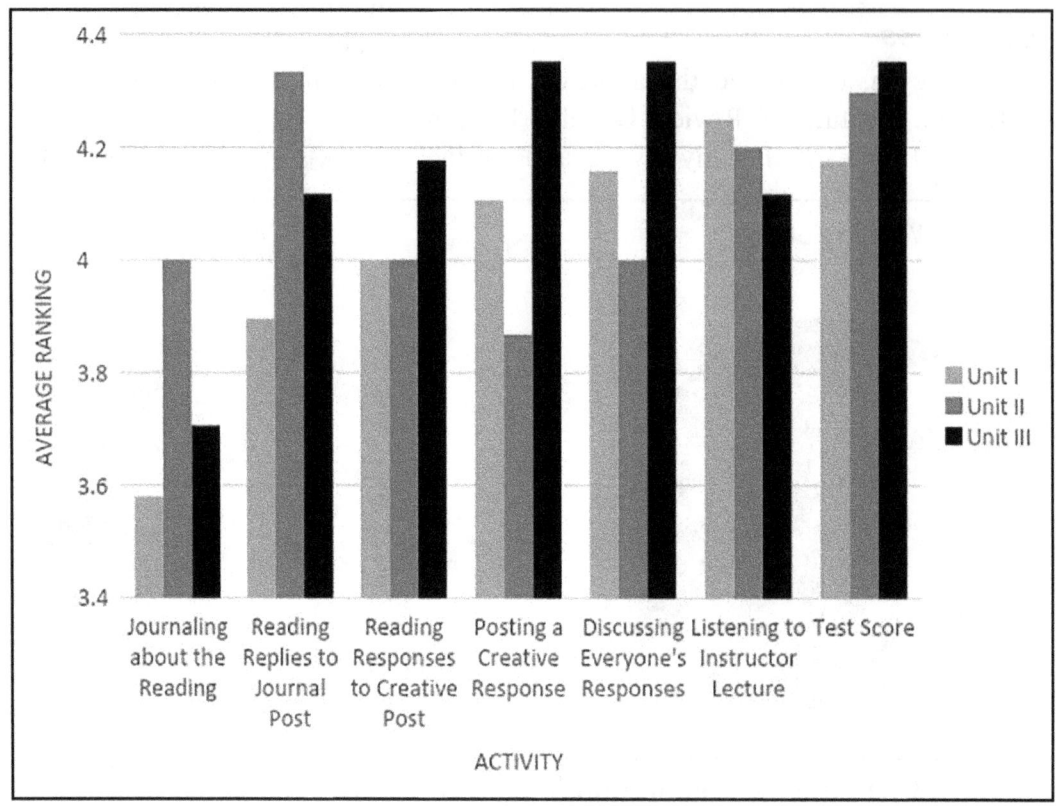

Figure 3. Changes in Learning Preference over the Course of the Semester

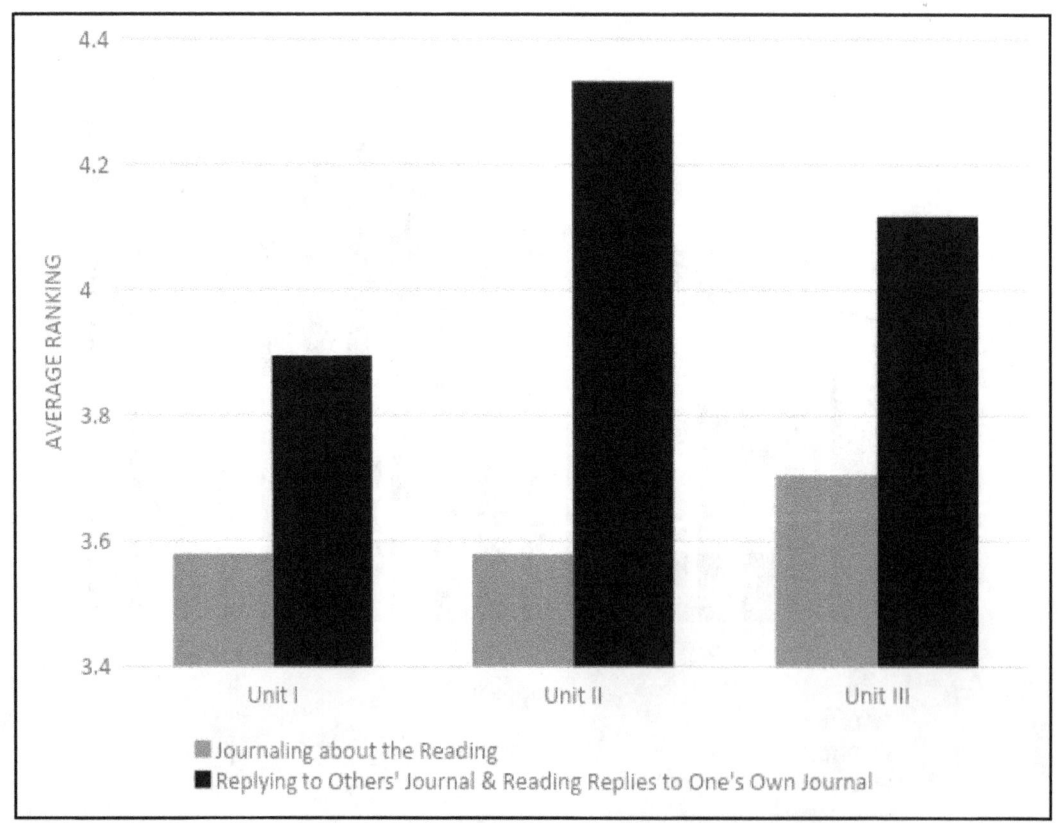

Figure 4. Preference for Interactional vs. Solitary Online Activity

lecture and discussion in the department's six core upper-division literature courses (for the survey see Appendix A).

To measure student learning, I used participants' scores on the unit tests, which weighed 25 objective questions and an essay equally. The essay allowed students to construct a thesis about the culture of the period and support it with two or three of the course readings. While the three unit tests combined were only weighted 30% of the course grade, they provided a relatively quantitative way of assessing learning progress.

At the end of the semester, I printed the questionnaires and entered the data into Excel. Using separate graphs for each unit, I numbered participants from lowest to highest test score recipient. Their rating for lecture and discussion appears on the y-axis, along with their score on the unit test. I then examined whether participants' ratings correlated with their assessed learning.

Discussion and Considerations
Interaction Enhanced Learning

The findings showed a consistent correlation between participants' ranking of class discussion and level of learning. As Figure 2 shows, the higher a student ranked discussion, the better the student performed on the assessment. The surveys following Unit II and III produced similar trendlines for discussion and learning (for the graphs see Appendix B).

Participants' open-ended comments reinforced the quantitative results. In response to the question, "What activity in the unit has helped make you more articulate?" the activity most frequently reported was discussion.

Preference for Interaction Increased

In addition to the results for individual participants as shown in Figure 2 and Appendices B and C, the data yielded class averages for each activity. The last three clustered columns in Figure 3 suggest that the group as a unit transformed its learning style over the course of the semester. As the class's inclination toward discussion rose, their tolerance for passive listening fell.

By contrast, Figure 3 shows that, among all activities, solitary journaling received the lowest rating. Moreover, according to Figure 4, which focuses on two online rather than in-person activities, participants ranked solitary journaling significantly

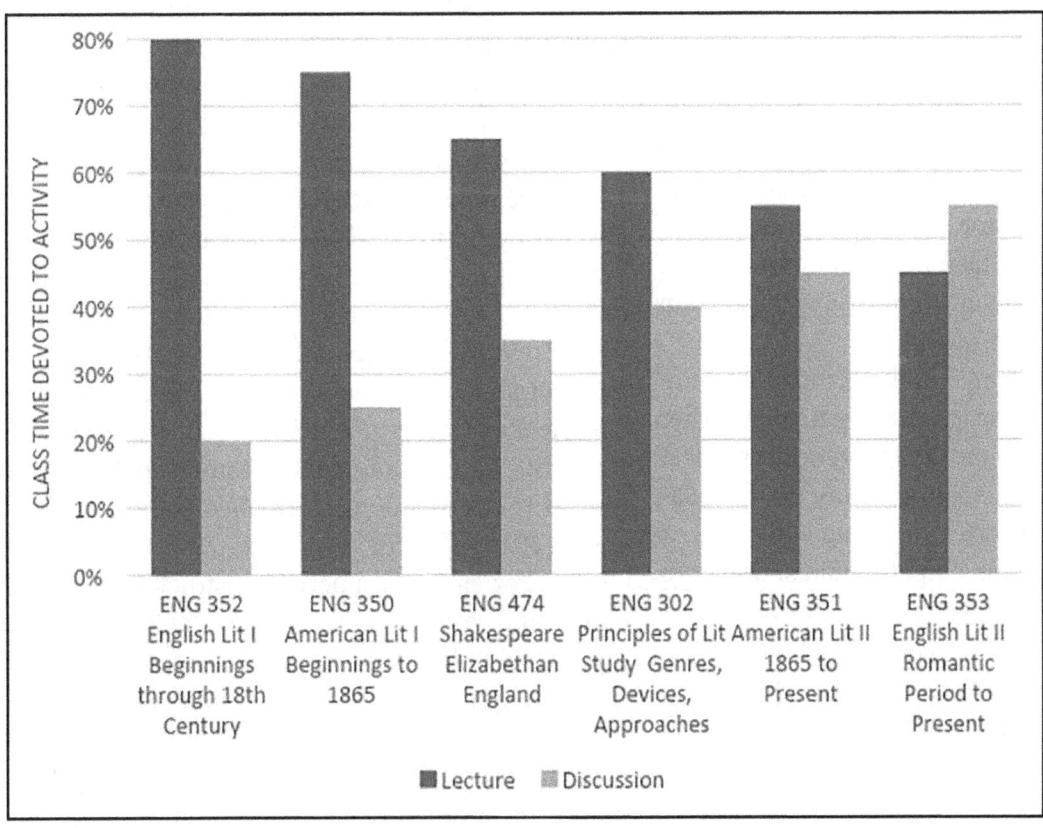

Figure 5. Class Time Spent on Lecture vs. Discussion

lower than virtual interaction. Students preferred reading their classmates' posts, replying to posts, and reading replies to their own post. In short, students preferred learning together. As Cillier has noted, this "connected" generation Z "expect a teaching environment in which they can interact in a similar way they do in their virtual worlds" (2017, p. 195).

The survey's open-ended questions, however, produced comments that acknowledged the value of solitary responses to the reading. In answer to the question, "What activity in the course has helped make you more articulate?" one student wrote, "definitely" the discussion board posts. Thus, even though solitary articulation ranked relatively low overall, more than one participant attested to the value of posting to forums; specifically, what helped the student was "the fact that you can't see anyone's posts before you do your own." This comment recognized that, however arduous, students needed to reflect on their own before coming together for group discussion. In short, as previous studies of today's students have shown (Cilliers, 2017; K. Mohr & E. Mohr, 2017, Seemiller & Grace, 2016), Gen Zers strongly prefer to leave the ivory tower of conventional learning for more collaborative and interactional approaches.

Traditional Course Format Persists

To provide an institutional context, participants estimated the use of class time in the upper-division English courses they had completed. Figure 5 ranks the literature courses for the major from low to high according to class time devoted to discussion. Lecture appears to prevail in most upper-division literature courses in the major.

According to Figure 5, today's instructors are devoting even more time to lecturing than in earlier decades. In addition to the student reporting, most of the instructors participating in my 2018 Pedagogicon workshop reported devoting over 50% of class to lecturing. Of the 28 participants, only two (science lab and media instructors) devoted more time to student talk and activities than to lecturing. This outcome duplicates the 1990 MLA finding that "There is little evidence . . . [that] faculty members have jettisoned traditional teaching methods in their upper-division literature courses" (Huber, 1992, p. 52).

Making the Adjustment

Baby Boomer, Generation X, and Generation Y instructors wish to bridge the gap with Gen Zers. To target their students better, they recognize characteristic Gen Z classroom behaviors (identified by my workshop participants in Appendix C) as cultural givens. Because Gen Zers avoid the routine of individual work and learn by doing, instructors must create opportunities for interaction. Instead of abandoning Gen Zers to "a crowded solitude" (Radaelli, 2015, p. 350), they must help them develop their emotional intelligence. They should encourage co-creation to harness students' desire for engagement. Because Gen Zers have a short attention span, instructors need to provide immediate response. About 11% of Gen Zers have experienced a diagnosis of ADHD. In addition, 32% of adolescents and 22% of young adults have an anxiety disorder that can inhibit concentration in stressful environments, such as the classroom (National Institute, 2018). By breaking the learning tasks into manageable segments, teachers can help students with this disorder. To address the high anxiety level of Gen Zers, teachers can keep their communication brief and limit themselves to mini-lectures.

Students learn by doing, not only by paying attention. To enable instructors to identify interactive/co-creative activities that engage Gen Zers, they can first acknowledge whether or not they spend too much time lecturing. After, they may choose to allot more time for discussion and student activities. Discussion fulfills students' need "to articulate their viewpoints to others, to recognize and contextualize others' viewpoints, and to hear their own viewpoints restated," which allows students to restate and reorganize information in relation to their own experiences (Bedetti, 2017, p. 112). According to Radaelli, "developing such interpersonal skills is pivotal for academic performance and career success" (2015, p. 346).

For each class period, instructors can plan and sequence short segments into a coherent learning arc, chunking content into "digestible bites" (Marzano, 2010, p. 83). For example, in my literature course, as Figure 6 shows, students engaged in a minimum of four interactions with the group before meeting in class. The online interactions encouraged multiple levels of learning. Sometimes the dialogic learning stemmed from discovering a likeminded sensibility, sometimes from accessing a classmate's unique perspective on the reading. When the tasks build to a coherent whole, students and their instructor leave the literature classroom tangibly elated.

If instructors "focus on the iGen strengths," they can cultivate the co-creative interactional environment that invites creativity (Sweet, Blythe, & Carpenter, 2018, p. 5). When instructors configure class periods to match Generation Z learning styles, their students' raised confidence, communication, and interpersonal skills will render them more agile and collaborative in the new workplace. The English major, in particular, will become the place where students "gain the riches that will be their intellectual capital for the rest of their lives" (Charon et al., 2009, p. 4). Rather than fading away, the liberal arts will bring about new meaning. They will help develop the skills students need to succeed at work and in life as well as become active, engaged members of their community.

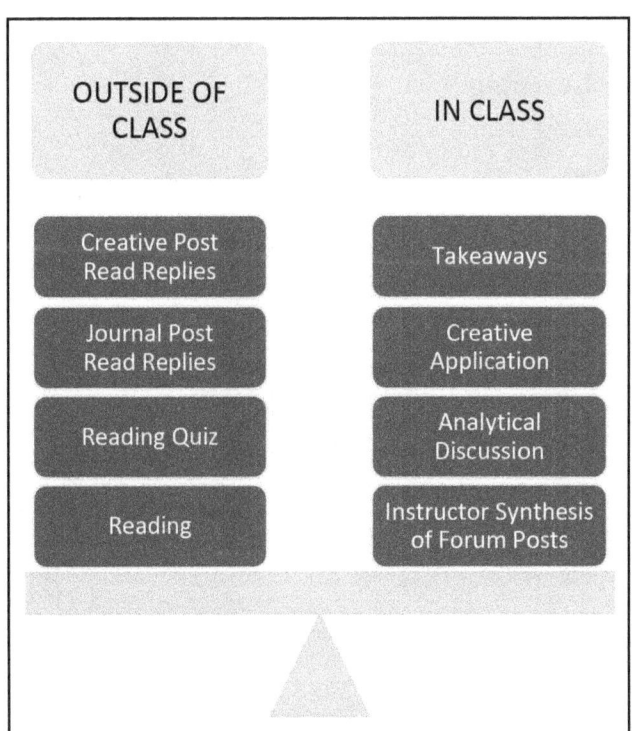

Figure 6. Sample Pre-Class Learning and In-Class Application

References

American Academy of Arts and Sciences. (2018a). Bachelor's degrees in the humanities. *Humanities Indicators*. Retrieved from https://www.humanitiesindicators.org/content/indicatordoc.aspx?i=34

American Academy of Arts and Sciences. (2018b). Racial/ethnic distribution of degrees in English language and literature. *Humanities Indicators*. Retrieved from http://www.humanitiesindicators.org/content/indicatordoc.aspx?i=242

Bedetti, G. (2017). Academic socialization: Mentoring new honors students in metadiscourse. *Honors in Practice, 13,* 109-140.

Beishline, M. J., & Holmes, C. B. (1997). Student preferences for various teaching styles. *Journal of Instructional Psychology, 24*(2), 95.

Buchanan, J. M. (2016). English education and the teaching of literature. *CEA Forum, 45*(1), 78-98.

Bureau of Labor Statistics. (2018) Writers and authors. *U.S. Department of Labor*. Retrieved from http://www.bls.gov/ooh/media-and-communication/writers-and-authors.htm

Charon, R., Christ, C. T., Graff, G., Gregory, M. W., Holquist, M., Marshall, D. B., . . . & Stewart, J. H. (2009). Report to the Teagle Foundation on the undergraduate major in language and literature: MLA Teagle Foundation Working Group. *Profession*, 285-312.

Cilliers, E. J. (2017). The challenge of teaching generation Z. *PEOPLE: International Journal of Social Sciences, 3*(1), 188-198.

Corrigan, P. T. (2017). Teaching what we do in literary studies. *Pedagogy: Critical Approaches to Teaching Literature Language Composition and Culture, 17*(3), 549-556.

Hayot, E. (2018). The sky is falling. *Profession*. Retrieved from https://profession.mla.hcommons.org/2018/05/21/the-sky-is-falling/

Houston, H. R., Keller, E. L., Kritzman, L. D., Madden, F., Mahoney, J. L., McGinnis, S., Monta, S. B., . . . Swaffar, J. (2001). Final report: MLA ad hoc committee on teaching. *Profession*, 225-238.

Huber, B. J. (1992). Today's literature classroom: Findings from the MLA's 1990 survey of upper-division courses. *ADE Bulletin, 101,* 36-60.

Kalata, K. (2016). Prioritizing student skill development in the small college literature survey. *CEA Forum, 45*(2), 54-85.

Laurence, D. (2017). The decline in humanities majors. *The Trend: The Blog of the MLA Office of Research*. Retrieved from http://stylemlaresearch.mla.hcommons.org/2017/06/26/the-decline-in-humanities-majors/

Marzano, R. J. (2010). Art & science of teaching. *Educational Leadership, 68*(4), 82-85.

Mohr, K. A. & E. S. Mohr (2017). Understanding Generation Z students to promote a contemporary learning environment. *Journal on Empowering Teaching Excellence, 1*(1), 9.

National Institute of Mental Health. (2018). Transforming the understanding and treatment of mental illnesses. *U.S. Department of Health and Human Services*. Retrieved from https://www.nimh.nih.gov/health/statistics/any-anxiety-disorder.shtml

Radaelli, E. (2015). Educating for participation: democratic life and performative learning. *Journal of General Education, 64*(4), 334-353.

Richardson, T. R., Kring, J. P., & Davis, S. F. (1997). Student characteristics and learning or grade orientation influence preferred teaching style. *College Student Journal, 31*(3), 347-355.

Seemiller, C., & Grace, M. (2016). *Generation Z goes to college*. John Wiley & Sons.

Sweet, C., Blythe, H., & Carpenter, R. (2018). Developing creative kids . . . and students. *The National Teaching & Learning Forum, 27*(2) 4-6.

Teach: Make a Difference. (2018). Kentucky teacher shortage areas. *Becoming a Teacher in Kentucky*. Retrieved from https://teach.com/become/teaching-credential/state-requirements/kentucky/#shortage

Appendix A
Survey on Course Format in Today's Upper-Division English Major

Questionnaire

Our learning outcomes in this upper-level literature course include
- to become familiar with the major writers and their works
- to understand how the writers fall into canonical literary periods
- to think, speak, and write effectively about the literature

Please Rank the Course Activities by Preference   Scale of 1 (lowest) to 5 (highest)

1) Writing a journal response to the reading   1   2   3   4   5

2) Posting and reading peer replies to the journal posts   1   2   3   4   5

3) Writing a creative post related to the reading   1   2   3   4   5

4) Posting and reading peer replies to the creative posts   1   2   3   4   5

5) Listening to the instructor lecture   1   2   3   4   5

6) Discussing everyone's response to the reading   1   2   3   4   5

Please Answer the Following Questions about Your Learning

1) Did you have a study partner/group?   Yes   or   No

2) Which activities contributed more to your learning?   Solitary   or   Interactive

3) In what ways have you become more articulate discussing the literature orally or in writing?

4) What activity in the unit has helped the most to make you more articulate?

5) Do you have comments, observations, and/or suggestions for enhancing your learning?

Please Answer a Question about Your Upper-Level Literature Courses

6) What percent of class time is devoted to lecture and discussion in each course?

Appendix B
Contribution of Lecture and Discussion to Learning in Unit II

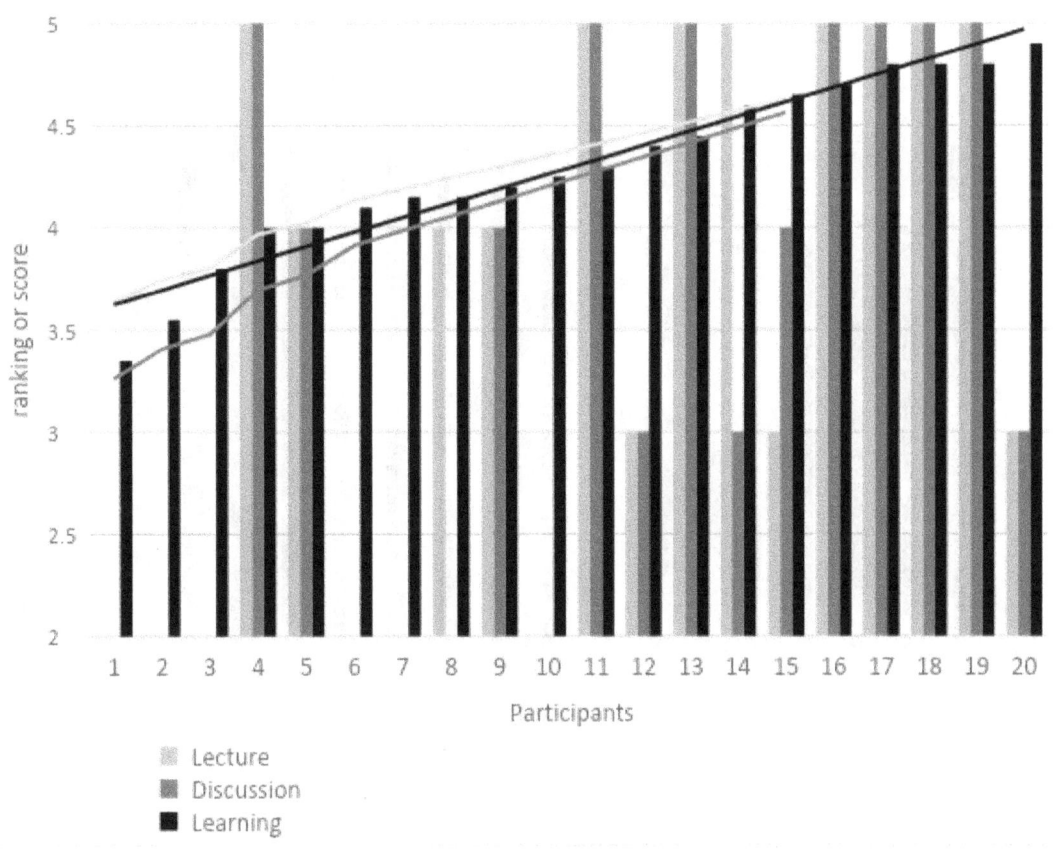

Appendix C
Contribution of Lecture and Discussion to Learning for Unit III

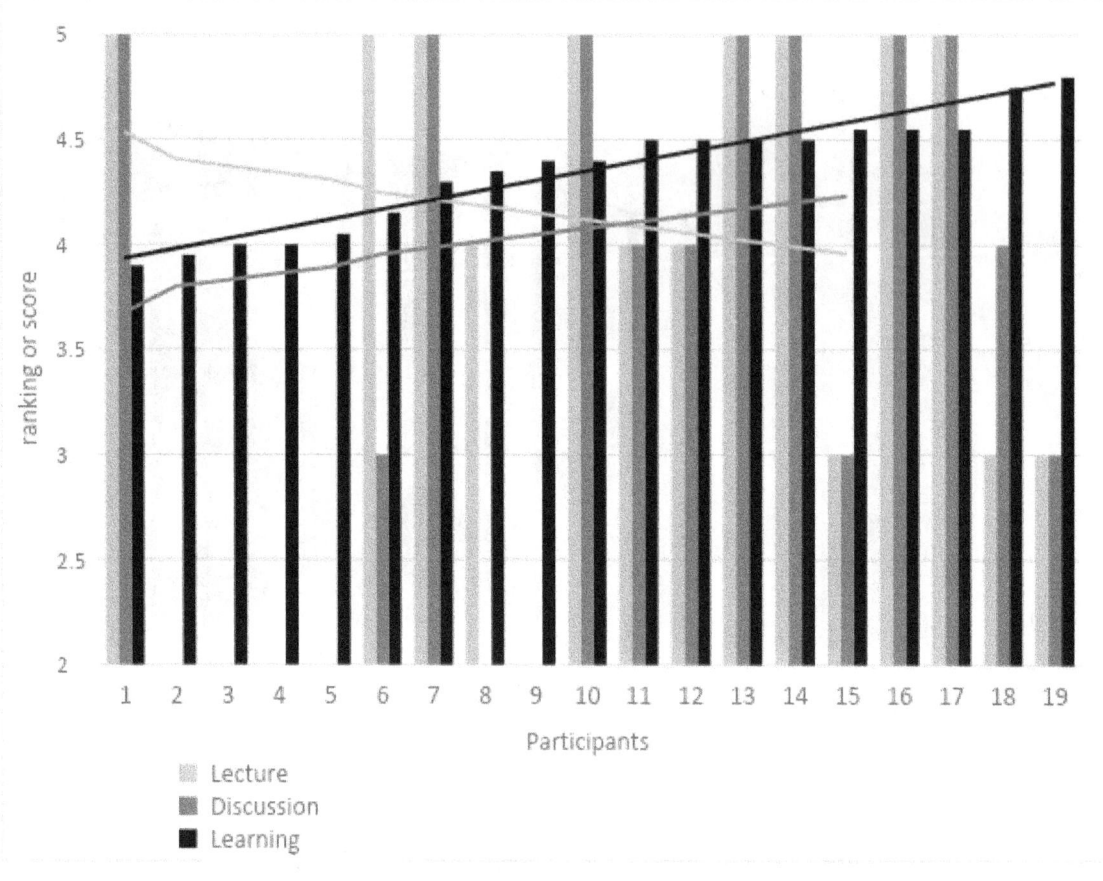

Appendix D
In-Class Behaviors of Generation Z Students

Digital Behaviors
- Look at screens
- Prefer digital communication
- Have phones out, texting
- Have headphones on
- Are constantly texting

Interpersonal Behaviors
- Don't ask or reply to questions
- Don't make eye contact
- Lack civility
- Don't understand audience
- Don't know each other

Personal Behaviors
- Are entrepreneurial
- Ask for concessions, entitled (grades, availability, rules)
- Exhibit anxiety, fear of failure, false bravado, easily offended
- Expect class to be easy, no effort
- Are open to group work, diversity

Communication Behaviors
- Write like they text
- Don't check school email
- Call instructor by first name
- Lack reading comprehension and vocabulary
- Have short attention span

Reinventing Student Engagement: The Role of In-class Simulation

Keri New, Catherine Edwards, Shannon Shumaker, & Brooke Bentley
Eastern Kentucky University

Classroom simulation and debriefing provide learners an opportunity to integrate didactic content into various clinical situations. This type of pedagogy encourages students to think critically and apply decision-making skills within a controlled, interactive environment. Debriefing, as part of the simulation process, enables students to evaluate their action through guided reflection.

Introduction

Effective teaching-learning strategies in higher education have a critical influence on student success (Kahu, 2013). Considerable debate exists on the intensity of student engagement that is needed to foster essential critical thinking that is necessary for effective learning (Schmidt, Wagener, Smeets, Keemink, & van der Molen, 2015). However, evidence suggests that student-centered teaching methodologies strengthen student engagement and predict student achievement (Abdel, Meguid, & Collins, 2017; Smith et al., 2005). As a result, there is a growing trend away from traditional didactic delivery of information in some areas of education. Thus, the use of novel teaching-learning approaches which support faculty-student interactions are essential in higher education.

In nursing education, there are resonant concerns related to a lack of "hands-on" activities in the classroom, limited clinical opportunities, and inadequate time for repetition of skills learned (Lindemulder, Gouwens, & Stefo, 2018). Yet, new graduates are expected to quickly become independent and competent professionals who are ready to undertake the complex care of clients within a diverse healthcare system. There is a national call for the preparation of future nurses to integrate competency while providing safe quality care (Dolansky & Moore, 2013). Therefore, effective teaching-learning strategies are critical to provide opportunities for student engagement where student-centered learning cultivates a safe environment for critical thinking.

Simulation is an effective teaching strategy that creates realistic environments to actively engage students in clinical reasoning (Sanko, 2017). The purpose of simulation is to provide a safe, controlled learning environment to practice skills, procedures, and processes (Keskitalo & Ruokamo, 2015). Its application has demonstrated utility in several disciplines including construction management, pharmacy, medicine, electrical and automotive engineering, psychology, and other dynamic interprofessional communication interactions (Benedict, 2010; Jaeger & Adair, 2012; Marken, Zimmerman, Kennedy, Schremmer, & Smith, 2010; Nembhard, Yip, & Shtub, 2009; Spalding & Rudinsky, 2018). Simulation is a valuable teaching method in nursing education as it mimics various "real-world" scenarios, in which a mistake may lead to a fatal outcome (Gaba, 2004). The students interact with a simulator and actors who role play patients and healthcare providers. Simulation-based learning portrays real life experiences and is provided in an interactive learning environment.

Context Active Learning

Classroom simulation incorporates active learning which is guided by the concept of the "flipped classroom." The flipped classroom is broadly defined as the interchange of traditionally experienced outside classroom activities implemented in the classroom as an interactive learning approach (McNally et al., 2017). Flipping the classroom is a pedagogical principle of learning that shifts the traditional didactic discourse toward a deliberate and collaborative student-centered application of classroom concepts (McLaughlin, White, Khanova, & Yuriev, 2016; Smith et al., 2005). This approach provides a framework for student engagement which broadens the student's method of inquiry, application, and evaluation of class content.

Overview of Classroom Simulation Development

There is a growing trend among educators to seek new and innovative uses of technology to engage students in the classroom (Damewood, 2016). Classroom simulation is an innovative use of technology which provides an engaging form of learning that enables students to visualize, analyze, and evaluate the clinical concepts presented to them. Simulation experiences provide the opportunity to replicate clinical events in a realistic manner (Lavoie & Clarke, 2017) by offering learning experiences within a safe and controlled environment (Kneebone et al., 2004). Therefore, classroom simulation is a valuable teaching strategy in a nursing curriculum. Each simulation experience follows the International Nursing Association for Clinical Simulation and Learning (INACSL) Standards of Best Practice Simulation^{SM} (2016) standards and is tailored to meet the needs of students.

Objectives

INACSL (2016) describe objectives as tools that will guide a simulation to achieve the desired outcomes in simulation. The objectives follow the S.M.A.R.T. acronym: S-specific, M-measurable, A-achievable, R-realistic, and T-timely. Objectives are leveled to meet the expected outcomes for simulation.

Scenario Development

Scenario development includes didactic faculty for the course, experts within the specialty, and the simulation coordinator. Scenarios are leveled within the curriculum to meet student learning outcomes. A simulation scenario is created to be realistic to patient care and supports the objectives developed for the students (INACSL, 2016).

Poll Questions

It is important to incorporate interactive poll questions into the development of the simulation. This interactive inquiry focuses on key objectives and encourages student engagement as the scenario unfolds. Simulations are paused at pivotal points to interject poll questions. The answers chosen by the majority of the class will guide patient care. Depending upon the selected answer, the patient's status may improve or deteriorate.

Observation Worksheet

The categories of the Creighton Competency Evaluation Instrument (C-CEI) were utilized to develop an observation worksheet (Todd, Hawkins, Parsons, & Hercinger, 2008). The worksheet provides areas for students to record patient assessment, communication, clinical judgement, professionalism, and patient safety simulation observations. Student are actively engaged by recording real time observations as the scenario unfolds.

Pre-Work Activities

Pre-work activities are required to prepare students for participation in the classroom simulation. An example of a pre-work activity is a voice-over PowerPoint presentation or an assignment with specific questions related to the scenario content.

Run Through

Prior to implementation of the planned scenario, it is recommended by INACSL (2016) to complete a run-through. Each faculty member participating in the simulation participates in the run-through of the scenario prior to implementing the scenario in the classroom. The run-through includes testing all technology and the rehearsal of each branch of patient care based upon selected answers from poll questions. This gives faculty the opportunity to ensure that each poll question and role play is an accurate representation of patient care.

Implementation

Faculty role-play patient care while the scenario is live streamed into the classroom. Poll questions are interjected throughout the scenario.

The care provided during the simulation is based on how the students answer each poll question. Scenarios continue to unfold as each question is answered by students.

Debriefing

Debriefing is an essential part of the simulation process and occurs with students immediately following the simulation. During the debriefing process, faculty led discussion allows students to reflect on the simulation experience (INACSL, 2016). Cantreel & Meakim (2014) describe the debriefing process as a time to respond to questions and collaborate with students to emphasize gold standards of care. Debriefing allows students to reflect on patient outcomes that are a direct result of their clinical decisions. It is recommended faculty utilize a script for effective debriefing (Mariani, Cantrell, & Meakim, 2014). A debriefing method that is widely used for healthcare simulations is Debriefing with Good Judgement (Rudolph, Simon, Rivard, Dufresne, & Raemer, 2007). The debriefing script includes three components: decompression, analysis, and summary. The decompression phase is a time for participants to state concerns about the simulation, and to review simulation objectives. During the analysis phase, questions are developed utilizing the advocacy/inquiry method to encourage student participation. For example, faculty may ask, "I observed... Can you tell me more about...". The summary phase is the time for students to reflect on scenario objectives and gold standards of patient care.

Student Evaluations

Student evaluations are completed immediately after the simulation activity. The Modified Simulation Effectiveness Tool (SET-M) is a commonly utilized instrument in healthcare simulation (Leighton, Ravert, Murda, & Macintosh (2015). This qualitative tool is used to collect data on student confidence, prioritization of care, effective communication, and patient safety.

Analysis of Blood Transfusion In-Class Simulation

In 2015, the Hospital Safety Score (2016) stated that hospital errors were identified as the third leading cause of death within the United States. Hospital errors are defined as preventable errors that include injuries, accidents and infections (The Hospital Safety Score, 2016). Therefore, the blood transfusion classroom simulation was developed to expose students to the process of safe administration of blood products and how to identify/intervene if a transfusion reaction occurs. Development of the simulation experience involves collaboration with the simulation coordinator to create objectives, outcomes, scenario, pre-work activities, interactive poll questions, debriefing script, and student evaluation.

Debriefing the Blood Transfusion Classroom Simulation

Directly after completion of the simulation, students participated in debriefing. Faculty who participated in the simulation scenario and the simulation coordinator led conversations to facilitate student critical thinking and reflection. The following are examples of questions asked during the debriefing:

- What did you observe about the pre-blood transfusion vital signs?
- What led you to make the decision to stop the blood transfusion?
- What did you observe about the level of professionalism and communication with the provider?

The class selected the correct answer to the majority of the interactive poll questions. The faculty further questioned the students regarding potential patient outcomes that would result from choosing incorrect poll answers. This type of questioning encouraged students to evaluate nursing care that could affect patient outcomes.

Student Evaluations for Blood Transfusion Simulation

Following the classroom simulation, students completed an evaluation of the simulation experience. Student evaluations revealed 98-100% of students either strongly agree or agree they were better prepared to respond to changes in their patient's condition and were more confident in the following areas: clinical decision making, prioritizing care, identifying interventions that foster patient safety, and recognizing effective communication with clients.

Discussion and Considerations

While student evaluations for the blood transfusion simulation were positive, findings are based on self-report and learner perception or descriptive qualitative analysis. This method of evaluation parallels most of the research in the literature supporting simulation as a teaching method for nursing education (Foronda, Liu, & Bauman, 2013). Evidence suggests simulation enhances clinical reasoning ability and supports the development of critical thinking (Dalton, 2015). When students were provided with a clinical scenario, interacted with role playing and mannequins, and participated in a debriefing session, they reported an increase in self-confidence to prioritize care (Zapko et al., 2015). Confidence is an important factor for nursing students, and those with high confidence levels are more likely to succeed in clinical performance and use clinical skills effectively (Lundberg, 2008). Hence, the combination of simulation exercises and roleplay improved student learning which subsequently improved confidence in critical thinking abilities.

The qualitative information yielded from student evaluations related to self-confidence and critical thinking ability is important, however, a more objective method is needed to measure the effectiveness of simulation-based learning. Limited research is available in this area. Student knowledge, as measured by post-test scores after a simulation-based resuscitation, improved as a result of the simulation (Malarvizhi, Glory, Rajeswari, & Vasanthi, 2017). Further data show that participation in simulation independently predicted student knowledge (Shinnick, Woo, & Evangelista, 2012). However, other evidence determined that improvements in student standardized test scores improved for some, but not all who participated in simulation (Glidewell & Conley, 2014). Thus, the impact of simulation on exam scores remains inconclusive.

The simulation team's next step is to incorporate assessment data from course exams and program readiness exams to measure outcomes of simulation-based learning. Data will be mapped using the electronic testing platform to link simulation related exam questions from pre-simulation to post-simulation semesters. For example, the simulation team observed 75% of students correctly answered an exam question prior to the introduction of a classroom simulation related to the exam question content. When the identical question was administered after the implementation of the simulation activity, 100% of students answered the question correctly. Longitudinal data will also be collected on the association between simulation content and student performance on the program exit exam. Further research is needed to establish the relationship between utilization of simulation and retention of learning based on quantitative outcomes.

References

Abdel Meguid, E., & Collins, M. (2017). Students' perceptions of lecturing approaches: Traditional versus interactive teaching. *Advances in Medical Education and Practice, 8*, 229–241. https://doi.org/10.2147/AMEP.S131851

Abelsson, A. & Bisholt, B. (2017). Nurse student's learning acute care by simulation- focus on observation and debriefing. *Nurse Education in Practice, 24*, 6-13. doi: 10.1016/j.nepr.2017.03.001

Benedict, N. (2010). Virtual patients and problem-based learning in advanced therapeutics. *American Journal of Pharmaceutical Education, 74*(8), 1–5.

Benner, P., Tanner, C. A., & Chesla, C. A. (1996). Expertise in nursing practice: Caring, clinical judgment, and ethics. New York, NY: Springer

Dalton, L. (2015). Using clinical reasoning and simulation-based education to "flip" the Enrolled Nurse curriculum. *Australian Journal of Advanced Nursing, 33*(2), 28–34.

Damewood, A. (2016). Current trends in Higher Education technology: Simulation. *TechTrends: Linking Research & Practice to Improve Learning, 60*(3), 268–271.

Dolansky, M. A., & Moore, S. M. (2013). Quality and safety education for nurses (QSEN): The key is systems thinking. *Online Journal of Issues in Nursing, 18*(3), 1–12. https://doi.org/10.3912/OJIN.Vol18No03Man01

Foronda, C., Lui, S., & Bauman, E. (2013). Evaluation of simulation in undergraduate nurse education: An integrative review. *Clinical Simulation in Nursing, e1-e8*. http://dx.doi.org/10.1016/j.ecns.2012.11.003

Gaba, D.M. (2004). The future vision of simulation in healthcare. *Quality Safe Healthcare, 13*, 2-10. doi: 10.1136/qshc.2004.009878

Glidewell, L., & Conley, C. (2014). The use of human patient simulation to improve academic test scores in nursing students. *Teaching and Learning in Nursing, 9*(1), 23–26. https://doi.org/10.1016/j.teln.2013.08.001

Groves, P. S., Manges, K. A., Cawiezell, J. S. (2018). Handing off safety at the bedside. *Clinical Nursing Research, 25*, 473-493. doi:10.1177/1054773816630535

Hallmark (2015). Faculty development in simulation education. *Nursing Clinics of North America, 50*, 389-397.

INACSL Standards of Best Practice: Simulation (2016). Retrieved from https://www.inacsl.org/inacsl-standards-of-best-practice-simulation/

Jaeger, M., & Adair, D. (2012). Communication simulation in construction management education: Evaluating learning effectiveness. *Australasian Journal of Engineering Education, 18*(1), 1–14.

Kahu, E. R. (2013). Framing student engagement in higher education. *Studies in Higher Education, 38*(5), 758–773.

Keskitalo, T., & Ruokamo, H. (2015). A pedagogical model for simulation-based learning in healthcare, *11*(2), 13.

Kneebone, R. L., Scott, W., Darzi, A., & Horrocks, M. (2004). *Medical Education, 38*, 1095-1102. doi: 10.1111/j.1365-2929.2004.01959.x

Lavoie, P. & Clarke, S.P. (2017). Simulation in nursing education. *Nursing Management, 48*, 16-17. doi: 10.1097/01.NUMA.0000511924.21011.1b

Leighton, K., Ravert, P., Mudra, V., & Macintosh, C. (2015). Update the Simulation Effectiveness Tool: Item modifications and reevaluation of psychometric properties. *Nursing Education Perspectives, 36*(5), 317-323. Doi: 10.5480/1 5-1671.

Lindemulder, L., Gouwens, S., & Stefo, K. (2018). Using QSEN competencies to assess nursing student end-of-life care in simulation: *Nursing, 48*(4), 60–65. https://doi.org/10.1097/01.NURSE.0000531006.94600.28

Lundberg, K. M. (2008). Promoting self-confidence in clinical nursing students. *Nurse Educator, 33*(2), 86–89. https://doi.org/10.1097/01.NNE.0000299512.78270.d0

Malarvizhi, G., Glory, H., Rajeswari, S., & Vasanthi, B. C. (2017). Outcome of clinical simulation on neonatal resuscitation in development of knowledge and skill among Baccalaureate nursing students at a selected nursing institution. *Asian Journal of Nursing Education and Research, 7*(3), 417. https://doi.org/10.5958/2349-2996.2017.00083.0

Mariani, B., Cantrell, M., & Meakim, C. (2014). Nurse educators' perception about structured debriefing in clinical simulation. *Nursing Education Percpectives, 35*, 330-331. doi: 10.5480/13-1190.1

Marken, P. A., Zimmerman, C., Kennedy, C., Schremmer, R., & Smith, K. V. (2010). Human simulators and standardized patients to teach difficult conversations to interprofessional health care teams. *American Journal of Pharmaceutical Education, 74*(7), 1–8.

McDougall, E.M. (2015). Simulation in education for health care professionals. *BC Medical Journal, 57*, 444-448.

McLaughlin, J. E., White, P. J., Khanova, J., & Yuriev, E. (2016). Flipped classroom implementation: A case report of two higher education institutions in the United States and Australia. *Computers in the Schools, 33*(1), 24–37.

McNally, B., Chipperfield, J., Dorsett, P., Fabbro, L., Frommolt, V., Goetz, S., ... Rung, A. (2017). Flipped classroom experiences: Student preferences and flip strategy in a higher education context. *Higher Education, 73*(2), 281–298.

Nembhard, D., Yip, K., & Shtub, A. (2009). Comparing competitive and cooperative strategies for learning project management. *Journal of Engineering Education, 98*(2), 181–192.

Rudolph, J., Simon, R., Rivard, P., Dufresne R., & Raemer, D. (2007). Debriefing with good judgement: Combining rigorous feedback with genuine inquiry. *Anesthesiology Clinics, 25*, 361-376. doi: 10.1016/j.anclin.2007.03.007

Sanko, J. S. (2017). Simulation as a teaching technology: A brief history of its use in nursing education. *Quarterly Review of Distance Education, 18*(2), 77–86.

Schmidt, H. G., Wagener, S. L., Smeets, G. A. C. M., Keemink, L. M., & van der Molen, H. T. (2015). On the use and misuse of lectures in higher education. *Health Professions Education, 1*(1), 12–18. https://doi.org/10.1016/j.hpe.2015.11.010

Shinnick, M. A., Woo, M., & Evangelista, L. S. (2012). Predictors of knowledge gains using simulation in the education of prelicensure nursing students. *Journal of Professional Nursing, 28*(1), 41–47. https://doi.org/10.1016/j.profnurs.2011.06.006

Smith, K. A., Sheppard, S. D., Johnson, D. W., & Johnson, R. T. (2005). Pedagogies of engagement: Classroom-based practices. *Journal of Engineering Education, 94*(1), 87–101. https://doi.org/10.1002/j.2168-9830.2005.tb00831.x

Spalding, C., & Rudinsky, S. (2018). Preparing emergency medicine residents to disclose medical error using standardized patients. *Western Journal of Emergency Medicine, 19*(1), 211-215. https://doi.org/10.5811/westjem.2017.11.35309

The Joint Commission (2017). Facts about patient centered communications. Retrieved from https://www.jointcommission.org/facts_about_patient-centered_communications/

Todd, M., Manz, J., Hawkins, K., Parsons, M., & Hercinger, M. (2008). The development of quantitative evaluation tool for simulations in nursing education. *International Journal of Nursing Education Scholarship, 5*, 1-17. Retrieved from http://www.bepress.com/injnes/vol5/iss1/art41

Zapko, K. A., Ferranto, M. L., Brady, C., Corbisello, A., Hill, D., Mullen, R., ... Martin, L. (2015). Interdisciplinary disaster drill simulation: Laying the groundwork for further research. *Nursing Education Perspectives (National League for Nursing), 36*(6), 379–382.

though individual contributions will vary, students should be expected to contribute to the team through full participation. Feedback must be provided in a timely manner, and team assignments should promote both learning and team development (Michaelson, Davidson, & Major, 2014).

Team-Based Learning: Teacher Preparation Course Application

Implementation of TBL into a language and literacy development course modeled aspects of this student-centered pedagogical approach by providing insight into the organizational format and participation in application-oriented activities aligned with units of study.

Team-Based Learning: An Opportunity to Model Student-Centered Learning in a Teacher Preparation Course

Michelle A. Gremp
Eastern Kentucky University

Quality post-secondary instruction must move beyond merely covering content to providing authentic opportunities for students. Implementation of Team-Based Learning into a language and literacy development course modeled aspects of this student-centered pedagogical approach by providing insight into the organizational format and participation in application-oriented activities aligned with units of study.

Introduction

Pedagogy is commonly understood as both the theory and practice of teaching; it is influenced by theories of learning and illustrated through teacher actions and student learning. Over the years, influences from behaviorist, cognitive, and constructivist theories of learning have influenced our educational system. From cooperative learning originating in the mid-1960s stressing the relationship between theory, research, and practice (Johnson & Johnson, 1999), to communities of inquiry and practice focused on doing and reflecting upon work in the field (Wenger, 1998), there is overwhelming agreement that quality post-secondary instruction must move beyond merely covering content to providing authentic opportunities for the application of concepts and the creation of solutions. One approach that seems poised to address this need is the Team-Based Learning (TBL) approach. Popularized by Larry Michaelson in the 1970s, TBL was originally implemented with medical students in order to engage them in open-ended problem solving activities as a means of preparation for professional practice (Walker & Guo Zheng, 2017).

Team-Based Learning Design

The design of TBL follows a fairly basic structure. The main focus is on the learner, with teachers acting as facilitators to provide guidance throughout the learning process. Students engage in problem-solving activities that allow them to use previous knowledge to gain new understanding. Learning occurs as teams share new experiences and solve relevant problems. Then, through the process of reflection after each problem-solving experience, students make judgements and modify their learning (Hyrnchak & Batty, 2012).

Team-Based Learning courses are designed around Modules, or units of learning, which focus on a specific topic and follow a three-step cycle. During the first step, students prepare for learning by reading assigned materials and completing a critical reading activity. In a continuation of assuring readiness, students next arrive in class and complete both an individual (iRAT) and identical team (tRAT) Readiness Assurance Test focused on major concepts of the readings. In-class grading of the team quiz provides immediate feedback. Clarification of any misconceptions is provided by the instructor in that same class or in a short lesson at the start of the next class. The final step of the cycle requires students to apply and extend knowledge they have gained from the readings through collaborative engagement in a problem-solving activity.

Successful implementation of the TBL paradigm is based upon intentional and specific design of four essential principles: team formation, accountability, feedback, and team assignments.

Teams must be created by the instructor to be diverse and permanent across the course of a semester. All students must be held accountable for both their individual and the team contributions.

Feedback must be provided from both the instructor and teammates and allows for the modification of learning. Finally, team assignments must promote a conceptual understanding of the content as well as the development of a strong team dynamic. Effective team assignments require that the problem at hand be significant (i.e. it should help to demonstrate the usefulness of the concept being learned), that the problem is the same for all teams, that teams apply content knowledge to make a specific choice related to concepts, and whenever possible conclusions should be reported simultaneously (Michaelson & Sweet, 2008).

Within the field of teacher preparation, the clinical model of learning has recently gained popularity. It is now common for teacher candidates to obtain hands-on classroom experiences throughout their programs rather than waiting until their culminating student teaching semester. Despite the similarity of clinical experiences with medical education, however, limited use of TBL in teacher preparation courses has been reported. In 2012, Hosier provided both qualitative and quantitative results after implementing a TBL approach in a teaching technology course. While a significant positive correlation emerged between iRAT scores mand final grades, the correlation between tRAT scores and final grades was even greater. Students indicated they enjoyed working in a team, but they did not like completing peer evaluations (Hosier, 2012). More recently, Walker and Guo Zheng (2017) implemented TBL for in-service teachers in a technology in education course in Singapore and reported positive feedback from students about the experience. In addition, just as Hosier reported, scores for team readiness assurance tests exceeded individual scores (Walker & Guo Zheng, 2017). In light of these positive results, implementation of the TBL approach in a variety of teacher preparation courses merits further investigation. If teacher preparation programs can provide teacher candidates with experience in this style of teaching and learning, these new teachers have the potential to transform the traditional education paradigm as they move into their own classrooms.

Applications to Course Design

While clinical experiences provide teacher candidates with some vital hands-on experiences and are becoming more common in teacher preparation programs, content-related coursework in still a necessary requirement. In these courses, hands-on learning seems to be forgotten and traditional lecture formats often prevail. Students quickly fall out of "teacher mode" and easily resume the traditional role of student as an absorber of information. They come to class without having read the required material or not understanding what they have read. This lack of preparedness on the part of the students naturally perpetuates the role of the teacher as talker or imparter of information in the classroom. Students sit in class and listen to facts the teacher presents to them, occasionally taking part if classroom discussions, but frequently multi-tasking (i.e. texting or playing a game on a mobile device or phone) instead.

If the traditional educational paradigm is ever going to change, a new generation of teachers must become adept facilitators and guides who provide problem-solving experiences in their own future classrooms. Therefore the decision was made to implement TBL in a language and literacy development course within a teacher preparation program. The intended goal was to increase student participation over traditional lecture courses and to provide insight into the design and experience of TBL that could later be replicated by students in their own classrooms. The principles of TBL guided the overall transformation of the language and literacy course, with minor adaptations being made to accommodate the unique spatial, time, and content-specific characteristics of the course. As each TBL principle was implemented, an explanation of the principle was provided to the students, therefore affording insight into the process of TBL design.

Team Formation

As previously noted, one major requirement of team formations is permanency. It is through continued interaction with the team members across an entire semester that relationships and shared accountability are developed. Equally important in team formation is the creation of diverse teams. Key elements considered included gender, intellectual abilities, personalities, and academic major. Students were asked to complete an informational survey on the first day of class which obtained these essential facts. Before the next class, the instructor sorted the surveys, pairing high and low GPAs, introverts and extroverts, upper and lower grade levels, and different areas of certification for the creation of highly diverse teams.

Accountability and Feedback

Preparedness must be ensured if TBL is to be successful, and as such reading readiness activities played a crucial role. Individual accountability was achieved through the reading response activities, individual readiness assurance quizzes (the term quiz was used in place of test in this course), and individual reflections following group projects, while team accountability was developed through contributions to the team readiness assurance quizzes and team projects, and results of peer evaluations. Reading readiness activities were designed in an open-ended format and were submitted prior to the start of each instructional unit. Students were allowed to choose between two options, a guided outline or written summary paragraphs. These readiness assurance activities were graded for completeness as well as accuracy. Upon arriving in class, students then took an individual quiz to guage their understanding and application of key concepts from the readings. They were permitted to use their completed readiness assurance assignment to assist with this. Upon completion of the individual quiz, teams then worked together to complete one team quiz which was identical to the individual quiz. Team quizzes were exchanged and graded in class, thus providing students with immediate feedback through access to the correct answers. Following the quiz a new Team Assignment prompt was introduced, and students used the remaining time and subsequent class periods (usually two or three) to formulate a solution to the given problem. Teams were required to present their "solutions" to the class on the final day of each unit, with all team members expected to share in presentation responsibilities. In conjunction with the team presentations, individual members were required to submit a reflection/analysis of learning. In this reflection students were asked to describe how elements of theirs and other teams' presentations related to key concepts of the unit. In addition, students were asked to provide an informal analysis of their team's performance and make suggestions for improvement. Presentations and reflection assignments were graded based upon a rubric, and personal comments were provided by the instructor. Two times within the semester, students completed peer evaluations requiring them to rate themselves and each teammate on the following four categories: reliability and responsibility, participation in work to solve the "problem," intellectual contributions, and contributions to the team presentation. Peer evaluations were presented in a rubric format, and detailed guidelines were provided stressing careful and fair judgements and restricting scores greater than 35 out of 40 for more than 2 people (including themselves) on any item, scores from all team members were compiled to create an average peer evaluation score. While specific comments remained confidential, scores from other teammates provided feedback on teammates' perception of each member's contribution.

Team Assignments

Perhaps the most crucial, and definitely the most challenging aspect of TBL implementation is the creation of meaningful team assignments. Successful team assignments align with Kolb's theory of experiential learning (Roberson & Franchini, 2014). This theory proposes that the experience of an action leads to reflection and is the first step in extracting conceptual understanding from content. As this extraction takes place, theories are developed and opportunities for experimentation take place. The repetition of this cyclical process allows learners to put into memory what they have learned so it can be applied in new situations. In essence, the learner goes beyond mastering information to truly interacting with it (Roberson & Franchini, 2014).

In the language and literacy course, team assignments were based upon existing course objectives. Prompts provided teams with information about specific (though not actual) children and required them to analyze components of language and literacy development, to make comparisons of typical speech, language, and literacy development to children with disabilities, to explain assessment procedures and results, and to formulate goals and outline evidence-based teaching strategies. The activities designed in this course met the criteria for providing a significant problem to be addressed and requiring a specific choice to be made relative to course content. However, while all teams were asked to address the same basic topic, different student information was provided for each team, meaning team problems were not exactly the same and presentations were not simultaneous. While departing from the strict guidelines set forth by Michaelson and Sweet (2008), this format allowed teams to hear other presentations and glean ideas for application of each unit's key concepts to numerous situations.

Learning Outcomes and Student Perceptions

Implementation of TBL in a language and literacy teacher preparation course for two semesters has proven to be successful. The depth of thought and completeness of the reading readiness activities indicated a deeper level of engagement with course content than was evidenced in previous versions utilizing a lecture format. The individual submissions allowed the instructor to evaluate the level of understanding for specific students and provide detailed feedback for clarification and improvement. Team presentations revealed a deep level of understanding and the ability to apply content information much earlier than with the previous course design. Class periods became productive work times where teams were actively engaged in applying concepts, often times seeking out additional resources beyond those presented in their text. The instructor's time was spent providing clarification and answering genuine questions for individual teams rather than standing in front of the entire class and delivering a monologue of facts, many of which students may have already known. Continued implementation in future semesters will allow for the collection of more objective performance data.

Student feedback was positive as well. When asked to comment on aspects of the course that helped them to learn, students overwhelmingly cited the readiness assurance activities. Specific comments indicated that completing the readiness activities required thorough reading of the material and that the act of writing the answers assisted in organization of the topics and led to better retention of the information. While this type of feedback was not entirely unexpected, additional comments were more surprising. Students commented that they liked the team work and the presentations; they found it beneficial to be learning from peers throughout the process; feedback from the instructor was helpful; and reflections forced them to think critically about their own efforts as members of a team and how to improve with each subsequent topic.

Considerations

TBL can be successfully implemented in a content area teacher preparation course. An abundance of evidence has shown its effectiveness for medical students and provides a roadmap of the design to guide the way. That does not mean that switching to this design is not without its challenges. Faculty must first overcome the feeling that they need to tell students everything that must be learned. Just as with the development of any new course, time must be spent upfront in designing application-oriented activities to align with units of study. Team size and the number of classes devoted to each topic must all be determined and may vary across content area. Modifications will likely be necessary from semester to semester as well. For example, after the first semester of implementing TBL it was obvious that students needed to be held accountable for the information being presented by other teams in addition to their own. Therefore, guided activities were created to ensure that students remained engaged and attentive to all presentations. Student feedback from the first semester also resulted in the revision of a number of team activities including providing different student information to each team. Yet despite the minor challenges associated with implementation, designing and refining a TBL class provides instructors with the same opportunity as the students: to apply content knowledge in real life situations, to reflect on course effectiveness, and to modify instructional design for improved learning outcomes.

Conclusion

Faculty in colleges of education must consider the need for providing authentic learning experiences in more than just clinical placement courses, and teacher candidates must have numerous problem-solving experiences that replicate their future classroom responsibilities. TBL is a good first step in providing these candidates with practice working as a team to apply content knowledge so they are equipped to provide meaningful learning experiences to their own students.

References

Hosier, A. (2012). When teachers are taught to learn: Using team-based learning as a first-time information literacy instructor. *College & Research Libraries News, 73,* 524-527. doi:https://doi.org/10.5860/crln.73.9.8828.

Hrynchak, P., & Batty, H. (2012). The educational theory basis of team-based learning. *Medical Teacher 34,* 796-80.

Johnson, D. W., & Johnson, R. (1999). *Learning together and alone: Cooperative, competitive, and individualistic learning* (5th ed.). Boston, MA: Allyn & Bacon.

Michaelson, L., & Sweet, M. (2008). The essential elements of team-based learning. *New Directions for Teaching and Learning. 116.* 7-27. doi: 10.1002/tl.330

Roberson, B., & Franchini, B. (2014). Effective task design for the TBL classroom. *Journal on Excellence in College Teaching, 25,* 275-302.

Walker, Z. M. and Guo Zhen, T. (2017) Adopting team-based learning for in-service teachers: A case study. *International Journal for the Scholarship of Teaching and Learning, 11,* 1-4. doi.org/10.20429/ijsotl.2017.110106

Wenger, E. (1998). *Communities of practice: Learning, meaning, and identity.* Cambridge: Cambridge University Press.

Best Practices for Engaging Introverts

Susan Weaver, Glenda Warren, & Chris Lockhart
University of the Cumberlands

Popular approaches to engage students through discussion, projects, and team-based learning ignore introverts' needs for time and space for reflection (Lueng, 2015). The resulting social landscape decreases satisfaction and presents barriers to success when participation is a grading criteria. The authors provide strategies that create productive learning experiences for introverts while modeling respect for individual differences in order to improve all students' self-awareness, confidence, and teamwork skills.

Introduction

The private, internal processing style of introverts is often confused with shyness or even a lack of knowledge, intelligence, or ideas (Cain, 2013; Lueng, 2015). The real difference is in how introverts and extraverts process information. Introverts need quiet space to organize their ideas and to plan their approach. Verbalization used by extraverts to talk through problems is perceived by introverts as overwhelming auditory interference (Lueng, 2015). Consequently, introverts leave a group interaction feeling drained while extraverts leave feeling exhilarated (Cain, 2013). The authors suggest adaptations to pedagogy that can bridge the processing styles of these two personality types to accommodate both introverts and extraverts.

Creating an introvert-friendly environment is important to overall student success because it meets the needs of all learners while addressing a cultural bias that favors extraversion as a sign of leadership (Leung, 2015). College professors usually show little sympathy for students who balk at in-class impromptu collaborative activities intended to foster engagement in the present and to cultivate professional skills for the future. In addition to value in creating a dynamic learning environment, collaboration ability has been identified as a 21st century skill (Saavedra, 2012) that is significantly correlated to career satisfaction (Lounsberry, Moffitt, Gibson, Drost, & Stevens, 2007). The National Survey of Student Engagement (NSSE) assesses the perceived presence of four indicators of engagement including collaborative learning, academic challenge, experiences with faculty, and campus environment (2015). Two of these, "Collaborative Learning," such as group projects, and "Experiences with Faculty," including discussing career plans, might be seen as incompatible with the internal processing style of introverts.

The premise of this paper is that one does not need to become an extravert to have positive collaboration experiences and skills. The following section shares adaptation of commonly used strategies to incorporate autonomy and private space for reflection needed by introverts.

Strategies

A professor's approach can make a difference in satisfaction and learning for both introverts and extraverts (Al-Dujaily, Kim, & Ryu, 2013). An early discussion on the topic by Schmerk and Lockhart (1983) reminds us that introversion – extraversion is a continuum rather than a dichotomy, and that most students have differing degrees of each. Lueng (2015) stated that accommodating both introverts and extraverts requires "attention to space, multiple intelligences, grouping strategies, choice, and flexibility" (p. 2). This section identifies common student issues of self-awareness, spontaneity, collaboration, and vulnerability.

Self-Awareness

Problem: Many students have not considered the importance of personality traits, learning preferences, or temperament much less how to value their own or those of others.

Strategy #1: A professor can use time before or after class to have informal conversations with introverted students to build rapport that can increase confidence and expose concerns.

Strategy #2: A proactive approach of using journals or reflection assignment challenges students to explore dimensions of personality, leaning style, and goals. Scales such as the *Kiersey-Bates*, (n.d.), *Myers-Briggs* (n.d.) and, most specifically, *Are You More Introverted or Extroverted?* with scale and applications (McIntyre, 2017) provide valuable insights that complement the *Visual, Auditory, Reading/Writing, Kinesthetic (VARK)* (2018) or Howard Gardner's *Multiple Intelligences Self-Assessment of Learning Preferences* (Edutopia, 2018). Incorporating reflections about learning styles and strategies enables students to think critically about individual inclinations and potential while developing academic skills of integrating data from the scales with application, analysis, synthesis, and evaluation. Results can be kept for discussion points in student advising meetings or expanded as vehicles for students to further explore implications of their styles beyond academic settings.

Spontaneity

Problem: Impromptu group discussions might be especially challenging for introverts who, by definition, do not want to jump into debates or discussions without reflection or preparation. Difficulty with this is exacerbated by extraverted students who like to reflect verbally.

Suggestion #1: Provide students with discussion questions or problems at least 24 hours in advance so that they can prepare. For example, math students might be assigned particular problems that they will have to put on the board. In other disciplines, students might be given case studies or a video with specific questions to address (DuBrowa, 2013).

Suggestion #2: Leung (2015) recommends one-on-one interaction rather than group discussions to provide a good experience for introverts. **Think, pair, share** provides individuals with time to process and formulate an answer before sharing. Simply, give one to five minutes to formulate an answer to a question then add an additional five to ten minutes for students to share with one other person with a reminder to change speakers at half time. This can be followed either by whole class discussion or shared ideas from a few volunteers. A modification that adds an additional layer of organization is to provide sticky notes for key ideas that each pair can attach to the wall or a flip chart with categories appropriate for the topic. This provides more specific role differentiation since one participant serves as a presenter. Another variation is the **gradual release model** that requires the professor to give information that the student uses in completing a worksheet or task then doing a group task using the information followed by time for individual effort and reflection to provide clarity and individual processing space in step two and four (Fisher & Frey, 2018).

Suggestion #3: **Fish bowl** can be valuable in addressing this concern. Have all students prepare from a common reading or reflection in advance. Place five to seven seats in the middle of the room. Students either volunteer or are assigned to all except for one seat in the inner circle to discuss or analyze a specific reading, issue, or topic. Those on the outside take notes on the points raised and on group processes. Anyone from the outside can take up the open seat. Similarly, anyone from the inside can move to the outside at any point to free up a seat for another volunteer (Bogush, 2011). This allows students time if they want to observe and reflect before committing to active discussion.

Collaboration

Problem: Projects require agreement on a topic, approach, and timeline all of which necessitate coordination, communication, and compromise. Failure is usually attributed to persons unwilling to do the work, but conversations with introvert's reveal that they prefer to commandeer the whole project because that is easier than trying to organize, negotiate, and insert accountability.

Suggestion #1: Jacobs (2017) reminds us that a group project does not mean that the group is in continuous interaction. An asynchronous example is the **flexible jigsaw project**, which gives each group member control over the development and presentation of his or her own portion of a topic while still having peers for reference if desired. Projects can be deconstructed into aspects such as background, events, relevant issues, leadership, or outcomes. If the project is an issue or policy analysis, then each student in the group can take position of a constituency about issues such as charter schools or alternative voting. Social science projects can be divided into parts such as cultural components with persons selected from a menu of religion, politics, health, and education. If a business class then each can take an aspect such as resources, market, or overhead (Boye, 2015). The flexible jigsaw approach gives each person individual control, responsibility, and accountability for his or her own section.

Suggestion #2: An alternative is **six hats** which is a strategy that assigns a specific role/hat to each person in the group who are charged with addressing a concern. These roles include red hat with focus on intuition hunches, feelings. White hat focuses on information, facts. Yellow hat focuses on positive aspects. Black hat focuses on cautions or difficulties. Green hat focuses on creative ideas or possibilities. Blue hat focuses on managing focus and giving summary. Students are told in advance what aspect of the discussion they will take and given access to the source material and prompts. This allows them to plan what they want to say in keeping with the assigned hat. The identified specific role provides an opportunity for positive collaboration (Litmos Heroes, 2014).

Vulnerability

Problem: Open interaction leaves a person feeling open to the possibility of being wrong or ridiculed. Technology can address fear of being wrong in two ways.

Suggestion: First, the use of ***polling technology*** such as clickers, Poll Everywhere, or simple colored paper voting can provide introverts with the processing space uninterrupted by group think (Sukanlaya, O'Connor, & Ali, 2017).

Second, Video content can be used to create a ***flipped classroom*** that provides foundation knowledge in advance so that all students have an opportunity to absorb the information and apply it before class discussion or activities. Honeycut and Warren (2014) offer ideas for a successful flipped classroom that incorporates introvert friendly strategies including writing prompts, opportunity to draw or map ideas, and a Strengths, Weaknesses, Opportunities, and Threats (SWOT) analysis (para. 11). These ensure that students potentially have time to process the material in advance.

Discussion

College students are faced with challenges given the need to adjust to multiple social landscapes and pressure to engage in collaborative activities in and out of the classroom. Accommodating the needs of introverts deploys pedagogy and resources that can lead to greater success and satisfaction. Many of the suggested approaches also develop metacognitive skills as each student learns to identify, cultivate, and appreciate his or her own approach to learning. The authors believe that this will lead to enhanced expectations of self and others.

References

Al-Dujaily, A., Kim, J., & Ryu, H. (2013). Am I an extravert or introvert? Considering the personality effect toward e-Learning systems. *Educational Technology & Society, 16*(3), 14–27.

Bogush, P. (2011, November 26). *Middle school fish bowl discussion.* [Video file]. Retrieved from https://www.youtube.com/watch?v=RwxnBv-dNBI

Boye, A. (2015). In consideration of effective group work. *Research and Teaching in Developmental Education, 30(1)* 60-62 Retrieved from http://www.depts.ttu.edu/tlpdc/Resources/Teaching_resources/TLPDC_teaching_resources/GroupWork.pdf

Cain, S. (2013) *Quiet: The power of introverts in a world that can't stop talking.* New York: Broadway Paperbacks

DuBrowa, M. (2013, Fall). Extroverts and introverts and 8am... Oh my! *Research & Teaching in Developmental Education, 30*(1), 60-62. Retrieved from https://www.jstor.org/stable/42802421

Edutopia (2018). Multiple intelligences self-assessment. George Lucas Educational Foundation. Retrieved from https://www.edutopia.org/multiple-intelligences-assessment

Fisher, D & Frey, N. (2018). Better learning through structured teaching: A framework for the gradual release of responsibility. Retrieved from http://www.ascd.org/publications/books/113006/chapters/Learning,-or-Not-Learning,-in-School.aspx

Honeycutt, B. & Warren, S. (2014, February 17). The flipped classroom: Tips for integrating moments of reflection. [Online blog]. Retrieved from https://www.facultyfocus.com/articles/blended-flipped-learning/flipped-classroom-tips-integrating-moments-reflection/

Jacobs, G. M. (2017, April). Introverts and cooperative learning. *IASCE Newsletter, 36*(1), 7-8. Retrieved from http://www.iasce.net/home/newsletters

Keirsey.com. (n.d.) What is your temperament? Retrieved from https://www.keirsey.com/

Litmos Heroes (2014, December 9). *What is six thinking hats?* [Video file]. Retrieved from https://www.youtube.com/watch?v=UZ8vF8HRWE4

Lounsberry, J., Moffitt, Gibson, L., Drost, A., & Stevens, M. (2007, June). An investigation of personality traits in relation to job and career satisfaction of information technology professionals. *Journal of Information Technology, 22*(2) 174–183.

Lueng, W. F. (2015, April). *Supporting introversion and extraversion leaning styles in elementary classrooms* (Master's thesis). Retrieved from https://tspace.library.utoronto.ca/bitstream/1807/68650/1/Leung_Winnie_F._201506_MT_MTRP.pdf

McIntyre, M. (2017). Are you more extroverted or introverted? Retrieved from http://www.yourofficecoach.com/coaching-resources/coworker-relationships/personality-differences/are-you-more-extroverted-or-introverted

Myers Briggs Foundation. (n.d.). My MBTI personality type. Retrieved from https://www.myersbriggs.org/my-mbti-personality-type/

National Survey of Student Engagement. (2015, July 23). Engagement indicators and -high impact practices. Retrieved from http://nsse.indiana.edu/pdf/EIs_and_HIPs_2015.pdf

Saavedra, A. R. & Opfer, V. D. (2012, October 1). Learning 21st-century skills requires 21st-century teaching. *Phi Delta Kapan,94*(2) 8-13). https://doi.org/10.1177/003172171209400203

Schmerk, R., & Lockhart, D. (1983, February). Introverts and extraverts require different learning environments. *Educational Leadership. 40*(5) 54-55. Retrieved from http://www.ascd.org/ASCD/pdf/journals/ed_lead/el_198302_schmeck.pdf

Sukanlaya, S., O'Connor, P. Ali, M. (2017). Using clickers to increase engagement in a large classroom. *Journal of Learning Design, 10*(1) 11-19. Retrieved from http://dx.doi.org/10.5204/jld.v9i3.292

VARK Learn Ltd. (2018). *The VARK Questionnaire. How do I learn best?* Retrieved from http://vark-learn.com/the-vark-questionnaire/

Going Back in Time: Designing Student Learning through Oral History Interviews

Melony A. Shemberger
Murray State University

Oral histories are student-centered learning opportunities that connect students more meaningfully to content. Any academic discipline could benefit from applying a historical context to any issue or topic being examined. This essay shares lessons from projects in two separate journalism and mass communications courses at a university in the Southeast. One project involved graduate research, in which public relations students were encouraged to find oral history files as part of their primary source list. The second project, in an undergraduate reporting class, was a yearlong, grant-funded oral history news endeavor about public education in Kentucky. Hopefully, these projects will inspire educators in various academic disciplines to integrate oral history interviews into their assignments and projects.

Introduction

Oral history interviews help historians and scholars to dig deep into studying the past and find information that deserves to be explored in greater detail. History teachers especially use firsthand accounts of historical time periods and events to help develop students' sense of history. Oral histories not only exist for history classrooms, but they are primary sources that help to enhance students' understanding of the historical period for any academic discipline. An oral history is a powerful pedagogical application to build historical understanding (Dutt-Doner, Allen, & Campanaro, 2016). In addition to gaining historical understanding, students are able to bring history alive by capturing personal stories and connecting with individuals to better understand their experiences and perceptions.

With this in mind, oral histories can serve as student-centered learning opportunities for a more robust connection to content. Any academic discipline could benefit from an opportunity to apply a historical context to any issue or topic being examined. This essay shares lessons from projects in two separate journalism and mass communications courses at a university in the Southeast. One project involved graduate research, in which students were encouraged to find oral history files as part of their primary source list. The second project, in an undergraduate reporting class, was a yearlong, grant-funded oral history news endeavor about public education in Kentucky. Journalism students used oral history as newsgathering and storytelling techniques in an effort to study the years before standardized tests became commonplace in classrooms. Audio files, transcripts, photographs of the interviewees, and news stories are stored on a website. Hopefully, these projects will inspire educators in various academic disciplines to integrate oral history interviews into their assignments and projects.

Types of Oral History

The body of scholarship within the oral history literature is extensive on how to incorporate oral histories into teaching and specific disciplines (Ritchie, 2003; Lanman & Wendling, 2006; Foster, 2013; Tobbell, 2016). Two instructional approaches to using oral history in teaching will be explained in this section because both were used in the projects.

One method is passive oral history, which uses audio or video recordings, transcripts, websites and other existing media files to connect the student or user with content. The second method, active oral history, focuses on the instruction of methodology and prepares students to be researchers to collect their own oral histories (Lanman & Wendling, 2006).

The incorporation of oral history into any assignment or project promotes student-centered learning and structures opportunities to reflect on student-created, rich insights. Under this framework, oral history interviewing can move students from being passive receivers of information to active participants who invest in their own discovery process. Technology use often is a component of student-centered learning because it allows for personalized learning. In the case of oral history, planned use of audio technology will guide the student to consider possible outcomes involving quality of sound. Therefore, the combination of oral history and technology empowers students to make decisions about their own learning and teaching.

Overview of Approaches

Oral history interviews were used in two university journalism classes—one a graduate public relations course in 2016 and the other an undergraduate course in 2017 and 2018. The graduate course applied passive oral history, while the undergraduate course used both approaches. Specific details about the assignments and projects are explained in the next sections.

Passive Oral History

For the graduate course, students studied the career of a communication professional, journalist or public relations executive and analyzed the individual's contributions. An important part of understanding any subject matter is to identify with a noted historical figure in the discipline or profession. Students wrote an analysis paper and created academic posters that were presented at the university's student research showcase near the end of the semester.

After instruction about oral history interviews, the students were encouraged to seek existing oral histories, or passive oral history interviews, about their chosen individual. Two students were able to locate audio files about their chosen media figures and incorporated oral history research into their work.

In the undergraduate course, oral history was applied as an innovative news-gathering and reporting method. Students completed a passive oral history assignment before conducting active oral history interviews for a class news project that focused on public education in Kentucky in the years before standardized testing became the norm.

Students completed a writing assignment that focused on passive oral history. The objectives of the assignment were to critique an oral history interview based on the material covered (e.g., interviewer talked too much, background noise created distractions) in the lectures and to identify best practices in conducting oral history interviews. This exercise served as the foundation for students as they completed their oral history news project.

Students accessed their choice of an oral history audio file online in the university library's collections and listened to the recording. In a reflective writing piece, students provided a summary of the topics discussed in the interview and a critical analysis dealing with the execution of the interview. This assignment allowed students to reflect on how to prepare and conduct oral histories.

Active Oral History

Active oral histories served as the main information-gathering technique for the undergraduate class news project. For fall 2017, Kentucky was chosen as the focus state because of its early emphasis on standardized testing as part of an overhaul of the public education system in 1990 based on the concept that all students have a right to receive an education that is based on equitable funding and resources. In spring 2018, the project focus expanded to Tennessee, Missouri, and Illinois.

Before conducting any active oral history interview, research of the historical timeframe in which the person being interviewed had lived or worked is crucial. To prepare for their upcoming interviews, students spent a week at the university's archives and collections libary. They toured the facility, learned about the resources available, and examined artifacts and documents relating to public education in the community and surrounding area.

In the fall semester, the instructor recruited interviewees to serve as oral history subjects. Basic information about the interviewees, such as their years of schooling in a K-12 public education system, was provided to students who then used the information to research educational issues and topics relevant to the subject's class years and plan questions to ask in the interview.

Two interviews were conducted in class using Tascam audio recording equipment purchased with a grant. Any device, such as a smartphone app, would work effectively. However, because the files in the project also served as a public resource, quality recordings were necessary. Two of the subjects came to the classroom for the interviews. The oral history interview with a third individual, who lived in another city far from the author's university, was conducted during class time via Zoom web conferencing. Both video and audio recordings were saved from this interview.

A student served as the official interviewer, who could be heard on the audio recording. At the start of each interview, the interviewer used a script to document the interview's details, such as the names of the interviewer and interviewee, date of the interview, and location of the interview—the formality observed by historians using oral history. During the interview, students tweeted to provide immediate updates on the project, took photos or wrote follow-up questions for the interviewer to ask. Each interview lasted approximately 25 to 30 minutes, the desired length for this project. After each interview, students wrote news stories based on the interview.

For the spring 2018 course, several changes and differences occurred. First, the project concentrated on oral histories of teachers. Each student selected an educator and conducted oral history interviews outside of class. Second, students had to transcribe their interviews. Third, a permission form signed by the interviewee was required. Fourth, the focus expanded past Kentucky to Missouri, Illinois and Tennessee, since three of the seven students enrolled in the spring course were from these states and more familiar with the educational systems in their home states.

Audio recordings, stories, photos, and other elements to document the interviews from both semesters were housed on a project website. These visible outcomes—the website and scholarly campus presentations—can be included in students' portfolios. In addition to the website, large-format posters were created. These included QR codes that were linked to the audio files and displayed throughout campus and in the community's public library. This positioned the undergraduate journalism project as a community engagement piece. Therefore, oral history presents itself as a student-centered approach to enhance community engagement.

Discussion and Considerations

By incorporating oral histories into class lessons and projects, students can study issues of today by placing people back into history, more so than a third-party source such as textbooks or other narratives. For the graduate students in particular, the use of oral history required them to evaluate sources critically, challenging them to recognize the limitations of each source they used and examine how that source complements the historical narrative. For this reason, the passive oral history method will be continued in the graduate curriculum. Educators are encouraged to incorporate passive oral history as much as possible to improve source evaluation and critical thinking and before students conduct active oral histories.

Oral history as a news-gathering and reporting technique also will be continued in the undergraduate reporting class. The topic of the in-depth class project might change, but the application of oral history will remain the constant because it has proven to be a student-centered approach to connect with the content. In addition, students achieve greater ease when using the more sophisticated audio equipment. Through oral histories, students can understand not only what happened in the past but also how those narrating the past interpreted events and issues. Plus, oral histories offer an opportunity for educators and students to give a voice to those who have not been heard or regarded on issues or topics.

In the scope of student-centered learning, oral histories woven into projects afforded students an opportunity to spend considerable time and effort on a topic over a period of time and to interact with diverse individuals. In the projects described in this essay, successful student-centered learning emphasized both creative and effective use of technology to meet students' learning goals. Students also have visible outcomes, the website and presentations, to include in their portfolios, demonstrate competency and share material that they collected with others. After having applied or conducted oral histories in an educational setting, students are more likely to collect oral histories that they find important. At best, oral histories can help students design their own learning, foster lifelong learners, and become more effective citizens.

References

Dutt-Doner, K. M., Allen, S., & Campanaro, K. (2016). Understanding the Impact of Using Oral Histories in the Classroom, *The Social Studies, 107*(6), 257-265, DOI: 10.1080/00377996.2016.1221792.

Foster, R. (2013). A storytelling training ground: Oral history in the journalism classroom. Retrieved from https://mospace.umsystem.edu/xmlui/bitstream/handle/10355/41121/analysis.pdf?sequence=2.

Lanman, B. A., & Wendling, L. M. (2006). Introduction. *Preparing the next generation of oral historians: An anthology of oral history education*, xix. New York, NY: AltaMira.

Ritchie, D. A. (2003). *Doing oral history: A practical guide*, 2nd ed.. Oxford, UK: Oxford University Press.

Tobbell, D. A. (2016). Teaching with oral histories. *Bulletin of the History of Medicine, 90*(1). 128-135. doi.org/10.1353/bhm.2016.0003.

First Steps in Qualitative Research

Aimee M. Cloutier & Ella L. Ingram
Rose-Hulman Institute of Technology

Faculty, especially those from science, technology, engineering, and mathematics (STEM) fields, often come to education research with the perspective that valid evidence is limited to quantitative data. However, qualitative research is increasing in prevalence and importance, as scholars and researchers come to understand how its approaches illuminate diverse perspectives and reveal unappreciated aspects of the student experience. In this paper, we introduce the core components of high-quality qualitative research, along with carefully selected resources, as a foundation for scholars who want to pursue qualitative research. We also reflect on the perspectives we brought to the study of qualitative research and our experience with a faculty development program that introduced qualitative research to STEM faculty. By increasing the scope of what constitutes valid, reliable evidence, qualitative research can inform scholars and educators about the student experience in new and enlightening ways. When faculty act on the lessons contributed from qualitative research, they can positively influence student learning.

Introduction

Research in teaching and learning provides considerable evidence that student-centered and interactive approaches work as well as traditional approaches and often better (Prince, 2004). Support for this finding emerges from both quantitative and qualitative methods. On the quantitative side, Hake (1998) provided a prime example, showing compelling evidence that interactive-engagement methods improve student performance. Meanwhile, the qualitative approach implemented by Magin and Churches (1995) demonstrated that peer tutoring provides educational benefits for both tutors and students. Excellent work from both quantitative and qualitative research methods confirms that student-centered and interactive approaches promote student success more than do instructor-centered approaches.

Research in student-centered teaching and learning can come from any discipline. Often educators conducting education research choose the research methods that align with the customs of their respective discipline. For example, an educator with a background in science, technology, engineering, and mathematics (STEM) topics may gravitate toward quantitative research approaches, whereas an educator in English literature might be inclined to choose a qualitative approach. However, in an ideal world, the research approach and methods should be dictated by the research question and not by the educator's discipline. Unfortunately, faculty performing education research may not have the knowledge, resources, or background to use effectively the approaches and methods that are not traditional in their discipline, or even to understand that better choices exist for particular research questions.

This research conundrum motivated our desire to write and share this work. We are two faculty members at a STEM college who, until recently, had little knowledge of or experience with qualitative research. Last year, we attended a workshop series that taught the basics of qualitative research approaches to qualitative research-naïve educators. We even did homework. Learning to conduct high-quality qualitative research transformed our approach to research design for education research (and, consequently, our perspectives on existing education research and the student experience of education). We feel that having knowledge of both qualitative and quantitative strategies gives us diverse and helpful tools for conducting research in student-centered teaching and learning, and we feel compelled to share this knowledge.

The remainder of this paper provides a launching point for those who are new to qualitative research. Throughout, we highlight example resources from a variety of disciplines. We briefly explain the core elements of high-quality qualitative research, namely epistemology, theoretical framework, methodology, and methods. We include our own reflections about the experience of learning to do qualitative research, which we use to frame the learning accomplished during the workshop and to highlight changes in our disposition toward qualitative research. Our goal is to empower research-active educators to explore and adopt qualitative research methods.

Aimee's Reflections

Prior to attending the workshop, the only research I had conducted used quantitative approaches and methods. I held the perception common to many STEM researchers that qualitative research is less rigorous or real, but conversations with colleagues who conduct qualitative research encouraged me to remain open-minded. Now, having corrected some of my misconceptions about qualitative research, I realize that neither approach is universally better. It is simply a matter of choosing the tool—qualitative, quantitative, or some combination of both—that is most appropriate for answering a research question.

Quantitative research approaches, for example, often aim for large-scale data collection that can be analyzed statistically and generalized. Whereas quantitative methods might determine whether a particular phenomenon occurs, qualitative methods, which typically prioritize text-based data collected on a smaller scale, might offer detailed insight as to why a phenomenon occurs.

Qualitative methods also capture the human experience in ways that quantitative methods miss. Researchers using quantitative approaches commonly assume that the data collected can be interpreted objectively and separately from the researcher's mindset and opinions. The perceptions and experiences of study participants, which in the case of research in teaching and learning can substantially alter data collection, might be considered factors or limitations that affect the results but are otherwise ignored. Qualitative approaches build assumptions and beliefs about the human experience into the research design, making them powerful for answering research questions in teaching and learning.

Epistemology and Theoretical Framework

The center of qualitative research is the combination of epistemology and theoretical framework. Together these features guide decision making in qualitative research. Epistemology describes the perspective on knowledge adopted by the researcher. As noted by Baillie and Douglas (2014), "Epistemology, then, describes the assumptions we are making about the nature of knowledge and what counts as evidence, with the aim of formulating or refining scientific research questions" (p. 2). More simply, epistemologies identify what researchers accept about how knowledge is created and managed. A researcher's epistemology is often so ingrained that it is unstated, although it is clearly present and influences the research. The epistemology adopted by the research influences all aspects of the research.

For example, imagine a team of researchers interested in learning benefits of extracurricular activities (Figure 1). If they adopted the empiricist epistemology, characterized by the acceptance of certain truth obtainable from observation and evidence, they would likely focus on features of student learning like exam performance or demonstration of skills (e.g., leadership). If instead the research team adopted the social constructionism epistemology, characterized by the belief that social interactions are the primary source of knowledge, they would likely focus on features of student learning. Such features include which students work together in what ways, how learning is transmitted from student to student, and the role of the advisor in leading students to learning via their interactions. This example illustrates how epistemologies differ in their assertion of who generates knowledge, how knowledge is validated, and what the utility of knowledge is, thereby affecting the direction, assumptions, and conclusions of qualitative research. Therefore, researchers must know which epistemology they are adopting. For researchers learning about qualitative research, a major first step is becoming conversant with various epistemologies and their consequences.

Once the researchers have identified their epistemology, they must select a theoretical framework. Theory is the lens through which an investigation is viewed. Merriam and Tisdell (2016) noted that theoretical framework influences "...the things we observe in the field, the questions we ask of our participants, and the documents we attend to are determined by the theoretical framework of the study. It also determines what we do not see, do not ask, and do not attend to" (p. 88). In social sciences, theory is "a set of interrelated constructs (concepts), definitions, and propositions that present a systematic view of phenomena by specifying relations among variables, with the purpose of explaining and predicting phenomena" (Kerlinger, 1986, p. 9). Researchers must select a theory to guide the investigation, so that the research can be aligned across all elements, thereby increasing the validity of the work and the community's confidence in its results (Walther, Sochaska, & Kellam, 2013).

For example, consider the question about learning benefits of extracurricular activities (Figure 1). If the research team adopted the theoretical framework of expectancy-value theory (a motivation theory; Eccles & Wigfield, 2002), they would explore features like students' expectations about their ability to succeed on projects associated with the extracurricular activity and the importance they place on the activity in furthering their academic success. If instead they adopted the theoretical framework of cognitive development (Perry, 1970/1998), they would explore features like how students describe their opinions, what role the advisor takes in knowledge delivery or creation, and if students explicitly incorporate values in their work.

Theoretical frameworks influence the researcher's attention to features of the experience. Therefore, the researcher must be intentional in the selection of a theoretical framework to confirm its alignment with the research question of interest. In the context of education research, several theories are common: Intersectionality, Cognitive Apprenticeship, Social Learning Theory, Communities of Practice, Intellectual Development, and Multimodal Communication among others (see Schunk, 2012 for comprehensive information). When taken together, epistemology and theoretical framework provide the boundary conditions within which the remainder of the research plan can develop.

Methodology and Methods

Although the terms methodology and methods are often used interchangeably, researchers treat them separately when conducting qualitative research. Methods refer to the data collection and analysis techniques used, whereas methodology represents the overall approach and theoretical justification for choosing those methods. When choosing a methodology, researchers deliberate about why a study should be designed in a particular way and how the methodology (and subsequently the methods) ties to the research question. Conducting this careful examination in the preliminary stages of research design allows the researcher to justify choices and to communicate this justification clearly.

The choice of methodology depends on, and connects strongly to, the researcher's theoretical perspective, and it informs the researcher's choice of methods. The choice of methodology also depends heavily on the research question and context of the study (Figure 1). Is the researcher acting as an observer or a participant? What kinds of artifacts will help to answer the research question effectively? Are the results intended to be generalizable, or should they focus deeply on a more specific case? Questions like these guide the researcher toward an appropriate methodology (see Table 1 for common methodologies and examples; see also Case & Light, 2011, Clough & Nutbrown, 2002, Creswell & Poth, 2017).

Like the methodology, the methods chosen depend heavily on how best to answer the research question. Quantitative research often aims to generalize results to a larger population. However, a researcher who wants to explore more deeply why a particular phenomenon occurs might benefit from considering qualitative methods. Rather than focusing on generalizability, these studies typically aim for transferability; although the research findings may not be generalizable to a larger population, it should be clear how they might be transferred effectively to new contexts. Qualitative methods often rely on analyzing textual evidence to gain insight, and appropriate data collection methods might include survey questions, interviews, focus groups, observation, and analysis of conversation (Borrego, Douglas, & Amelink, 2009).

Ella's Reflections

I have been reading more work using qualitative methods that helped me understand the stories behind the numbers and the stories that numbers

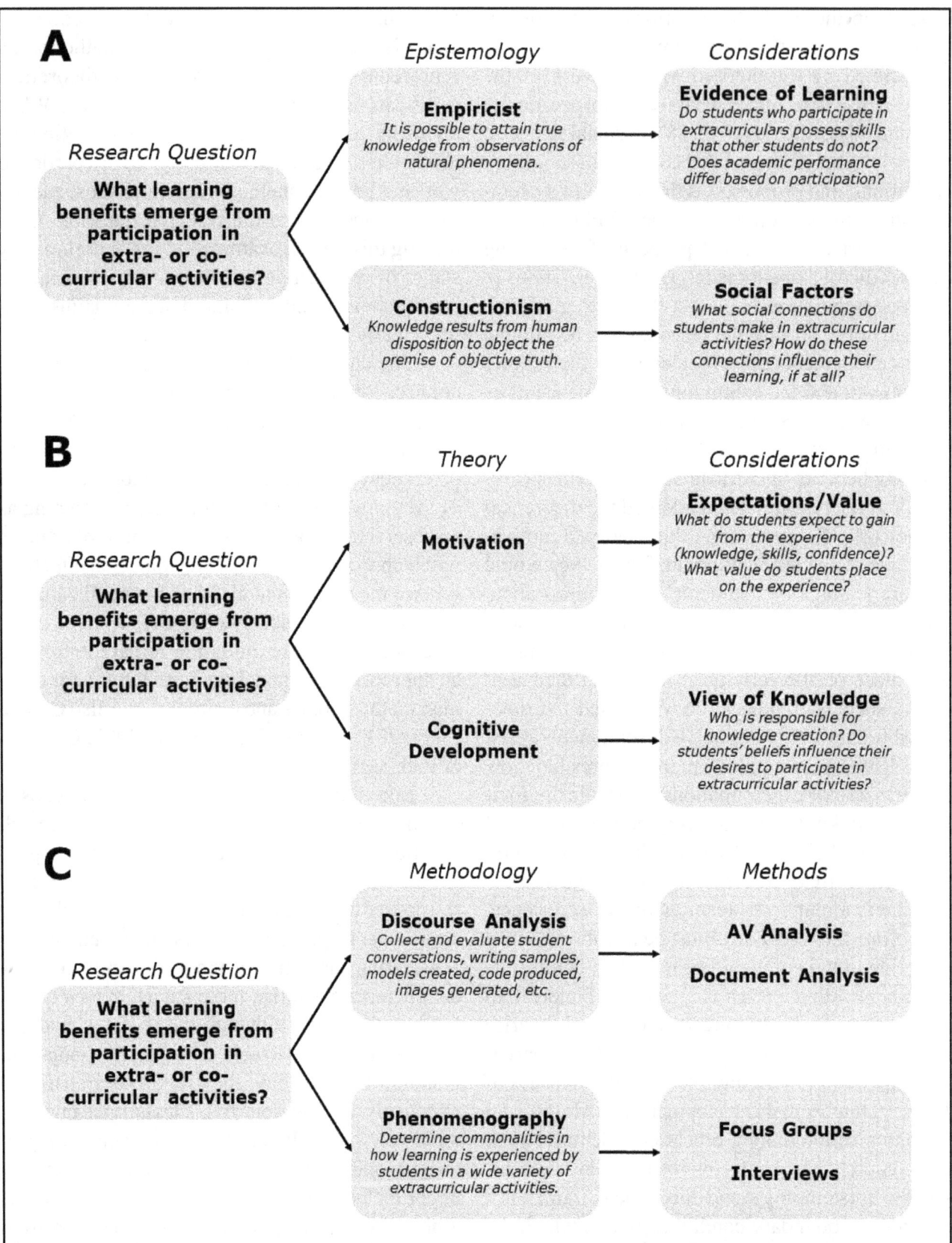

Figure 1. Different choices influence how qualitative researchers construct their research project. A) Example decisions related to epistemology; B) Example decisions related to theory; C) Example decisions related to methodology.

can't tell. I attended the workshop to learn the right way to do qualitative research. The facilitator asked "What assumptions about knowledge do you make when doing research?" I didn't have an answer; of course, I had assumptions, but they were unarticulated. Learning that researchers specify the epistemology of their work transformed my understanding of qualitative research. A second question was "What theories frame your work?" I didn't understand that theory could be explicitly selected. What I thought of as stories, I now view as data emerging from fundamental assumptions about reality. In addition, I understand the complex-ness of qualitative research, although I do not understand the complexities of qualitative research.

More questions developed: How can one ask good questions (in either qualitative or quantitative research)? How does my question fit into a larger context? What is the practical significance of answering my question? What claims do I want to make about the results or products of my research? Prior to a discussion of "good questions", I didn't see the parallel between my teaching students about good practice in quantitative research methods in biology and good practice in qualitative research in education. Now, the connections are obvious, and extend beyond just questions to include research practices that lead to high-quality work. Moving forward, I will identify how beliefs, perspectives, and experiences influence the work. In addition, I will create alignment of epistemology, theoretical framework, methodology, and methods. In learning more about high-quality qualitative research, I discovered multiple resources that address how researchers can affirm qualitative research quality (e.g., Mays & Pope, 2000 [health care], Seale, 1999 [social science], Walther et al., 2013 [engineering education]). I anticipate using these resources in a campaign of self-education to improve my qualitative research skills.

Table 1. Common methodologies in qualitative research, with examples from various disciplines.

Methodology	Description	Example
Case Study	Using a single example or a selected few examples to explore a phenomenon	Zogaj, Bretschneider, and Leimeister (2014) researched the challenges of crowdsourcing in software development, using a start-up company as the unit of analysis.
Discourse Analysis	Analyzing language in all forms to understand context and meaning	Hardy and Phillips (1999) studied how political cartoons describe society's views on immigration, with a focus on the Canadian refugee system and the language surrounding refugee status.
Ethnography	Capturing behaviors and representational artifacts as a means to understand society and culture	Bucciarelli (1988) investigated the acts and culture of engineering design to characterize the processes of design.
Action Research	Engaging in research by and for educators to cause change	Bommarito (2016) evaluated the experiences of a mentor and five students as they collaborated on a research project, with a goal of improving mentorship in writing.
Autoethnography	Connecting the author's experience and perspectives to larger cultural experiences and norms	Neville-Jan (2003) used her lifetime of unexplained and unmanaged pain to frame a consideration of how pain is conceptualized in social and medical settings.
Phenomenology	Discovering lived experience through the subject's words, to understand rather than explain	Holder, Jackson, and Ponterotto (2015) explored the experiences of Black women in corporate leadership, to model the coping strategies used to manage racial microaggressions.

Discussion

This paper is our message of hope to others like us that developed as scholars in a quantitative research tradition: you, too, can learn to use qualitative research approaches in education research, and you should. Becoming literate in the core basics, and quickly, is possible (and note, we'd say the same thing about quantitative research: informative research can use simple paired t-tests, no MANCOVA needed). Although the learning curve is steep at first, learning by doing is a sure method of skills development. To support this effort, we carefully selected resources that are accessible and information-rich, with the idea that they would serve as a mini-course for interested scholars. Through this paper, we hope to empower future education researchers who right now would be considered naïve qualitative researchers.

Education research—both qualitative and quantitative—describes the key features of high-quality learning experiences (e.g., high-impact practices, see Kuh, 2008). The shape and nature of these experiences is made vivid through qualitative research. It captures the lived experience of students, reveals the nuance and personal aspects of education, and reconsiders what counts as knowledge and whose knowledge counts. Because of its ability to describe the student experience, qualitative research represents an opportunity for research-active faculty of all stripes to inform student-centered educational practices.

References

Baillie, C., & Douglas, E. P. (2014). Confusions and conventions: Qualitative research in engineering education. *Journal of Engineering Education, 103*(1), 1-7.

Bommarito, D. V. (2016). Collaborative research writing as mentoring in a U.S. English doctoral program. *Journal of Writing Research, 8*(2), 267-299.

Borrego, M., Douglas, E. P., & Amelink, C. T. (2009). Quantitative, qualitative, and mixed research methods in engineering education. *Journal of Engineering education, 98*(1), 53-66.

Bucciarelli, L. L. (1988). An ethnographic perspective on engineering design. *Design Studies, 9*(3), 159-168.

Case, J. M., & Light, G. (2011). Emerging research methodologies in engineering education research. *Journal of Engineering Education, 100*(1), 186-210.

Clough, P., & Nutbrown, C. (2002). The Index for inclusion: Personal perspectives from early years educators. *Early Education, 36*(Spring), 1-4.

Creswell, J. W., & Poth, C. N. (2017). *Qualitative inquiry and research design: Choosing among five approaches* (4th ed.). Thousand Oaks, CA: SAGE Publications.

Eccles, J. S., & Wigfield, A. (2002). Motivational beliefs, values, and goals. *Annual Review of Psychology, 53,* 109-132.

Hake, R. R. (1998). Interactive-engagement versus traditional methods: A six-thousand-student survey of mechanics test data for introductory physics courses. *American Journal of Physics, 66*(1), 64-74.

Hardy, C., & Phillips, N. (1999). No joking matter: Discursive struggle in the Canadian refugee system. *Organization Studies, 20*(1), 1-24.

Holder, A. M. B., Jackson, M. A., & Ponterotto, J. G. (2015). Racial microaggression experiences and coping strategies of Black women in corporate leadership. *Qualitative Psychology, 2*(2), 164-180.

Kerlinger, F. N. (1986). *Foundations of behavioral research* (3rd ed.). New York, NY: Holt, Rinehart, Winston.

Kuh, G. D. (2008). High-impact educational practices: What they are, who has access to them, and why they matter. Washington, DC: Association of American Colleges and Universities.

Magin, D. J., & Churches, A. E. (1995). Peer tutoring in engineering design: A case study. *Studies in Higher Education, 20*(1), 73-85.

Mays, N., & Pope, C. (2000). Assessing quality in qualitative research. *British Medical Journal, 320*(7226), 50-52.

Merriam, S. B., & Tisdell, E. J. (2016). *Qualitative research: A guide to design and implementation* (4th ed.). San Francisco, CA: Jossey-Bass.

Neville-Jan, A. (2003). Encounters in a world of pain: An autoethnography. *American Journal of Occupational Therapy, 57*(1), 88-98.

Perry, W. G. (1970/1998). *Forms of intellectual and ethical development in the college years: A scheme,* New York, NY: Holt, Rinehart, and Winston; 1998 reprint San Francisco, CA: Jossey-Bass.

Prince, M. (2004). Does active learning work? A review of the research. *Journal of Engineering Education, 93*(3), 223-231.

Seale, C. (1999). Quality in qualitative research. *Qualitative Inquiry, 5*(4), 465-478.

Schunk, D. H. (2012). *Learning theories: An educational perspective* (6th ed.). Boston, MA: Allyn & Bacon.

Walther, J., Sochaska, N. W., & Kellam, N. N. (2013). Quality in interpretive engineering education research: Reflections on an example study. *Journal of Engineering Education, 102*(4), 626-659.

Zogaj, S., Bretschneider, U., & Leimeister, J. M. (2014). Managing crowdsourced software testing: A case study based insight on the challenges of a crowdsourcing intermediary. *Journal of Business Economics, 84*(3), 375-405.

Incorporating Soft Skills for Student Success

Lynda N. Donathan & Anthony T. Dotson
Morehead State University

A goal of any educator is to prepare a well-rounded student to be successful in the classroom and beyond. To facilitate effective student learning, it is important to identify essential soft skills inside and outside of the classroom and ways to incorporate these skills. This paper reinforces how a focus on soft skills in professional education can influence success in today's workplace.

Introduction

Studies show that in today's society there is a significant deficiency in basic soft skills. Soft skills include communication skills, listening abilities, and character traits that allow individuals to work and perform well with others (Cimatti, 2016). According to Richard Fry of Pew Research Center, more than one-in-three American labor force participants (35 percent) are millennials, making them the largest generation in the labor force (Fry, 2018). Students who later become employees sometimes lack in these basic skills. Soft skills are tacit in our communications in the academic environment. They are essential for success in the workplace.

In today's classroom, these skills are essential for success. Literature suggests that soft skills equal student's and then employee's "emotional intelligence, which reflects one's ability to interact with others in a positive manner" (Brown, 1999). Possessing excellent soft skills equates to positive student interactions, leading to excellent customer service, something that concerns all employers during tough economic times. The goal of this paper is to identify student soft skills, and to examine tools for dealing with personal and professional soft skills. Our primary focus will be to demonstrate how basic soft skill tools can improve the student's ability to transition from student to successful employee. Specifically, we will demonstrate the added benefit of the student's ability to interact in a positive manner with others in the academic setting, which will provide a happier learning environment. Minimal modifications to the existing classroom can evolve to an environment where students obtain essential soft skills, in addition to hard skills, that allow them to transition from student to a more successful employee.

Purpose

The purpose of this paper is to identify essential soft skills and to examine tools for promoting those skills in the academic setting. By deliberately planning and including soft skill tools within an academic course, improvement should be seen in the learner's ability to transition from student to successful employee in the work setting. A literature review using several electronic databases to locate articles provided a basis for the presentation. The definition chosen for this article for soft skills is "the character traits and interpersonal skills that characterize a person's relationships with other people (Educational Technology and Mobile Learning)."

Personal Soft Skills

Personal soft skills represent those skills that need to originate outside of the office or job. These personal skills should develop first and some refer to them as "fixing the loose ends". Examples of personal soft skills include personal appearance, sleep/time management, transportation, school schedule, childcare, second jobs, and finally legal issues/divorce/custody. There are many tools, or suggestions, that can apply to the skills that are relevant to both students and future employees. These tools should be applied to personal needs outside of the classroom or workplace. For instance, there should be a plan in place for potential surprises such as a sick child or back up transportation in case of vehicle breakdowns. There should be a plan in advance for such things as childcare and an adequate sleep schedule. Scheduling should also be in place to ensure that second jobs do not interfere with the individual's class time or main occupation. Appropriate scheduling is a strong skill as long as you adhere to the schedule. Procrastinating on tasks or personal problems will affect a schedule and in turn will negatively affect an individual's academic course work and employment.

Professional hard skills describe an individual's knowledge and occupational skills gained in the course of professional education (Educational technology and mobile learning, 2015). Soft skills and hard skills work hand in hand to ensure success as a student and future employee. The website *Educational Technology and Mobile Learning* identified ten key skills for the 21st Century worker. The professional skills include leadership, collaborations, adaptability, global citizenship, critical thinking abilities, communication, information analysis and synthesis, productivity and accountability and an entrepreneurial spirit. Developing and refining these skills within professional education programs should foster a seamless transition of college graduates to the workforce (Loup, Kornegay, & Morgan, 2017).

The transition from student to employee is commonly a challenging process, as contexts and demands change. Some basic soft skills if followed, can ease the transition. The first is the concept of company culture. Tory Johnson is the founder and CEO of Women for Hire, a major company that specializes in virtual career expos and conferences for women. She speaks about company culture being described as the atmosphere or vibe of a workplace (Women for Hire, n.d.). This would include the work style and values of the company. A perspective employee should learn about a company's culture. To do this an individual can answer some basic questions. Examples of these questions include: What do you want me to accomplish? What tools do I need to be familiar with to be successful? To whom do I address questions? What communication method is preferred?" In order to be accepted into the culture of an organization, a person needs to be service oriented. Working with co-workers and having a positive demeanor is key to the service provided to an organization. This means professionalism is necessary. Professionalism consists of positive attitude, flexibility, networking, good work ethic and avoiding negatives. Negative people, conversations, and gossip should be avoided. Work etiquette is also important to the culture of a place of employment. Being respectful of others, being punctual, appropriate dress, and demonstrating basic manners are components of work etiquette. There are basic rules to follow to ensure that you maintain etiquette. These include observing boundaries, being accountable, asking questions, respecting the time of others, fulfilling commitments, paying attention, and being genuinely nice.

There are other skills that need to be developed. To be successful in the work force, a person needs to be an indispensable worker. To be indispensable to a work place, some skills are essential after learning the culture of the organization. Communication is a valuable skill for a person to learn. This includes dialogue with co-workers. Asking co-workers for their ideas in a respectful and kind way is a great way start this process. After initiating a dialogue, a person can improve communication by following directions, practicing active listening, and giving credit to others when appropriate.

It is also important to be a problem solver. Creative problem solving is valuable to employers. Taking a risk and creating new ideas is a positive attribute for an employee. However, it is important to be respectful in communicating your ideas to others. A perspective employee should also be goal oriented. When setting goals, one should be reasonable and set obtainable goals. It is also a good idea to keep records of you progress obtaining your goals.

Tools to Improve Student Soft Skills

In the classroom setting, students can learn how to observe boundaries and be respectful by following policies in course syllabi and handbooks. The educator can add civility, etiquette, attendance, and netiquette policies to these documents. A student can be held accountable by following academic course policies for assignment and project submission. The educator can develop assignments and group projects that require the students to attend to detail, respect time limits, and ask questions. By adding group-work, the educator can demonstrate to the student that fulfilling their commitment to the group is essential to a successful group project. The more difficult part of the challenge for faculty is to provide continual opportunities for students to practice the soft skills that are critical to success in the workplace. And finally, the process must be interesting, fun, and meaningful for a generation that thrives on instant gratification, instant information sharing and an almost all-encompassing obsession with social media (Loup, Kornegay, & Morgan, 2017). Table 1 summarizes soft skills that should be considered in the academic setting as developed by or compiled from Investopedia.

Summary

The academic educator must consider the relationship of professional coursework with preparing graduates for successful careers. Consideration of soft professional skillsets is critical in developing tomorrow's leaders. A general knowledge of basic soft skills can bolster collaboration, motivation, and cooperation in the academic setting as well as the professional setting. Obtaining these skills can make the education experience more meaningful for the student and make the transition to the workforce more successful. By intentionally focusing on soft skills needed for communication and leadership in academic coursework, we will better prepare our students in the transition to success in the employment setting.

References

Brown, B. L. (1999). Emotional intelligence: Keeping your job. *ERIC Clearinghouse on Adult, Career, and Vocational Education.* Center on Education and Training for Employment. College of Education, Ohio State University. ED 1.310/2:435041

Cimatti, B. (2016). Definition, development, assessment of soft skills and their role for the quality of organizations and enterprises. *International Journal for Quality Research, 10*(1) 97–130.

Fry, R. (2018, April 11). Millennials are the largest generation in the U.S. labor force. In Pew Research Center Fact Tank Blog. Retrieved June 30, 2018 from http://www.pewresearch.org/fact-tank/2018/04/11/millennials-largest-generation-us-labor-force/

Loup, C., Kornegay, J., & Morgan, J. (2017). Career exploration and soft skills: Preparing students for success, *Connecting Education and Careers. 92*(1), 14-17.

Educational Technology and Mobile Learning (2015, April 15). Retrieved from https://www.educatorstechnology.com/2015/04/10-essential-skills-for-21st-century learners.html

Investopedia (n.d.). Retrieved from https://www.investopedia.com/articles/personal-finance/111015/overlooked-skills-you-need-succeed-work.asp

Performance Management Counseling. (2013, November 21). Top 10 soft skills for job hunters. In PMCounseling Blog. Retrieved from https://pmcounseling.wordpress.com/2013/11/21/top-10-soft-skills-for-job-hunters/

Women for Hire. (n.d.). Tory Johnson Founder, CEO. Retrieved from http://womernforhire.com/about_us/tory_johnson_founder_ceo/

Table 1: Examples of Soft Skills

Examples of Soft Skills: Top 10 Soft Skills for Job Hunters
1. Strong Work Ethic Are you motivated and dedicated to getting the job done, no matter what? Will you be conscientious and do your best work?
2. Positive Attitude Are you optimistic and upbeat? Will you generate good energy and good ill?
3. Good Communication Skills Are you both verbally articulate and a good listener? Can you make your case and express your needs in a way that builds bridges with colleagues, customers and vendors?
4. Time Management Abilities Do you know how to prioritize tasks and work on a number of different projects at once? Will you use your time on the job wisely?
5. Problem-Solving Skills Are you resourceful and able to creatively solve problems that will inevitably arise? Will you take ownership of problems or leave them for someone else?
6. Acting as a Team Player Will you work well in groups and teams? Will you be cooperative and take a leadership role when appropriate?
7. Self-Confidence Do you truly believe you can do the job? Will you project a sense of calm and inspire confidence in others? Will you have the courage to ask questions that need to be asked and to freely contribute your ideas?
8. Ability to Accept and Learn from Criticism Will you be able to handle criticism? Are you coachable and open to learning and growing as a person and as a professional?
9. Flexibility/Adaptability Are you able to adapt to new situations and challenges? Will you embrace change and be open to new ideas?
10. Working Well Under Pressure Can you handle the stress that accompanies deadlines and crises? Will you be able to do your best work and come through in a pinch?

Retrieved from https://www.investopedia.com/terms/s/soft-skills.asp

Engaging Agents: Students as Class Facilitators for Academic Articles

Tanya Robertson
University of Louisville

Reading an academic article takes time, practice, and the recognition that it is a learned skill. It is a transferable skill necessary for students' academic careers as well as their professional and personal lives. This essay encourages instructors to consider using students, agents, as class facilitators to teach academic articles. A class facilitation article assignment can be useful in any discipline and at any level. Using academic articles as a running narrative that links the coursework helps to address the problem of students compartmentalizing their assignments instead of recognizing the relationship linking everything from small activities to major projects.

Introduction

Reading an academic article takes time, practice, and the recognition that it is a learned skill. Not only is this a skill necessary for students' academic careers, it provides a foundation (a transferable skill) for engaging with texts that is important for their professional and personal lives as well. Academic reading "serves to position future academics in disciplines (at both national and international levels) and to shape their trajectory within wider interdisciplinary fields" (Hill & Meo, 2015). This essay encourages instructors to consider using students, agents, as class facilitators to teach academic articles. A collaborative class facilitation article assignment can be useful in any discipline and at any level. Articles progress in difficulty throughout the semester and weave a thread between all of the course materials, promoting deep learning and remembered knowledge. In other words, using academic articles as a running narrative that links the coursework helps to address the problem of students compartmentalizing their assignments instead of recognizing the relationship linking everything from small activities to major projects.

Pedagogically, the class facilitation article assignment lends itself to discussions of internal diversity *within* cultural groups and *between* cultural groups more broadly. According to Wilfred (2017),

> In the collaborative learning environment, the learners are challenged both socially and emotionally as they listen to different perspectives, and are required to articulate and defend their ideas. In so doing, the learners begin to create their own unique conceptual frameworks and not rely solely on an expert's or a text's framework.

As agents, students bring their own experiences and backgrounds to the readings, share those various interpretations, and can therefore recognize that each individual will view the same text through their own specific cultural lens.

Addressing the Needs of Student Readers

Because this assignment works at any level for any type of course, this essay will explain it as an overall strategy while using real examples from writing studies courses. The class facilitation assignment aligns with many university and department goals for programs across campus. It can address everything from critical thinking skills and sense of purpose to social awareness and cultural diversity. The goals set by departments and programs in the university setting often include demonstrations of critical thinking through writing. In the case of research and writing courses, students are required to produce a certain amount of revised and edited texts for a variety of audiences using multiple genres. For example, a student in an English 101 or English 102 course may be required to perform academic research and compose informative and argumentative projects that synthesize a number of sources. Often, these sources will be from academic journal articles and books related to their disciplines or course topics.

Students approach these texts based on past experiences. Even if those strategies were not successful, they continue with those practices because they have never learned another method. It is even more of a challenge for instructors with students who have never been exposed to college level writing such as recent high school graduates. These students lack the understanding that there exists a difference between how they learned to read in high school or GED courses and what is required of them as college-level readers. According to Hermida (2009), "most first-year students lack academic reading skills, especially because university-level reading great differs from high school reading. Thus, most students employ non-university strategies to read academic texts, which results in students taking a surface approach to reading" (p. 20). That surface approach leads to missed connections between the readings and the course goals, short-term knowledge that is forgotten as soon as the exam or project is completed, and, especially for block courses, the absence of knowledge transfer.

Assignment and Agent Strategies

The strategy to address these concerns is the establishment of student teams to teach a series of academic articles—they become agents in the active learning process. Students are assigned to class facilitation collaborative teams (CFCTs) a few weeks into the semester. That allows for time to get to know students and see how they might work together. Each collaborative team is assigned an article and will teach that article to the class on their assigned date. The amount of theory present in each article, the difficulty in concepts, the length of the article, and the complexity of the author's language increase as the semester continues. CFCT one gets the most accessible, shortest article and the last collaborative team, team five in this example, gets the longest and most difficult article.

CFCTs can teach the article any way they see fit. Often, they will approach the assignment based on their past experiences in the classroom. The lesson must include key terms and definitions from the text as well as discussion questions for the class. The teams can design a presentation, prepare a handout, upload an assignment to Blackboard, plan in-class group work, or any activity that they feel will help their classmates understand the article. For a 75 minute class, the facilitation must last at least 55 minutes. That allows for an introductory reading quiz and for instructor wrap-up at the end.

Additionally, the collaborative team will submit a reading grid of the article. Generally, they will include the reading grid as part of their facilitation lesson. The reading grid is part of the deeper reading required of the CFCT. It must include an APA citation and an explanation for each of the following points: problem (what problem or issue is the author trying to highlight?), purpose for writing (why is the author writing the text?), old knowledge (what does the author say that professionals, teachers, scholars, and others used to think about the topic of the article?), new knowledge (what is the author's thesis?), methodologies used (how does the author approach the text and/or organize the argument?). The reading grid assignment takes the place of the annotated bibliography. The grid submitted as part of the class facilitation assignment is shorter than the one for the main reading grid assignment.

The facilitating team also submits any handouts, presentations, and assignments used throughout the facilitation along with the completed reading grid. These items are uploaded to the Blackboard coarse shell. Their classmates are responsible for coming to class having read the article and must be ready to participate in whatever lesson the facilitating team has prepared. All students will take a short reading quiz (not a comprehension quiz) over the article at the beginning of class. The CFCT is required to take the quiz. This is one way to verify that all students on the team read the assigned article and actively participated in designing the presentation.

The role of the instructor during the facilitation is two-fold. First, it is to act as a student in the class. This includes raising a hand to ask questions, joining discussion groups, and completing any of the assigned activities. Simultaneously, the instructor is taking grading notes and monitoring class participation and engagement. The second role of the instructor is to ensure that the team teaching the article is not providing incorrect or inaccurate information regarding the reading. To do this, the instructor may raise his or her hand and clarify points or add an additional way of understanding or interpreting the reading. At this point, the instructor may also make a connection to other readings, assignments, and concepts.

Example Class Facilitation Assignment

The articles themselves demonstrate what credible, ethical research looks like, how to find it, how to critically read academic and professional publications, and how to synthesize that information into an informative work. In these example writing courses, students analyzed the rhetoric of human rights running throughout *The Hunger Games* trilogy by Suzanne Collins. The courses were writing and composition studies courses, not literature courses or literary theory courses and the focus was on the use of rhetoric and how writing is used to advocate and persuade.

Students read book one of the trilogy and each one chose a human rights topic displayed in the book and based off of their personal interests or academic objectives. As a general example, a criminal justice major might examine the use of public floggings as a form of punishment. A military science major might study the use of child soldiers in civil wars. A pre-med student may focus on access to medical care and the use of folk medicine. All of the work for the remainder of the semester used their chosen topic. They performed extensive research on their topic and produced several projects reflecting the ability to think critically about their subject matter including research posters, literature reviews, public service announcements, and advocacy websites.

CFCT one, was assigned an article written by a language arts instructor about the use of *The Hunger Games* trilogy to teach social action. It was eight pages long with fairly accessible language. CFCT one taught about one month into the semester. CFCT five was assigned an article that discussed the issues of race and racism that resulted when the book was produced as a film and African American actors were cast in some of the roles. That article was 21 pages long and contained much more rhetorical and social theory as well as more complex language.

Discussion and Considerations

As part of the active learning that takes place with this assignment, students in the example courses engaged in the problem solving and critical thinking process on their own. Having an internal group discussion about what they would present as part of the facilitation assignment helped individual students to get clarification on sections where they were confused. If students needed additional help understanding complex concepts, theory or language, they could request an instructor meeting (as a group or in part). Most often, facilitating teams said they *had it all worked out* and did not require assistance. Although a printing and copying offer was presented, they made their own handouts and presentations and never asked to have those things done for them. They maintained that for any issues that they faced, they were able to solve them as a team. It was the idea sharing and discussions with each other that helped them to grasp difficult concepts in order to be able to bring them to the class.

What occurred by mid-semester was that the facilitating groups began to take the role of the course instructor and included the connections to previous class assignments and lectures as part of their presentations. They regularly made statements such as *"do you remember when we did this or learned about that in class? Well, this is an example of that or this is kind of the same thing or this author talks about that."* The confidence of being able to make those connections led to another positive outcome of the class facilitation assignment – student involvement.

One of the assignment guidelines is that all members of the team must actively participate in the presentation and discussion which means that even the shier students must engage with the class and demonstrate their understanding of the readings. During the example courses, sometimes these students began the presentation by simply reading a slide but at some point they started to adlib a little or chime in to clarify a term or concept. Since they were presenting as a team, they felt more comfortable talking to the class and because they realized they could tie things into previous lessons, they had the confidence to do so. On the classroom side of things, students who typically were more reserved and quiet in class participated in the CFCT discussions. The people standing at the front of the room were their peers and friends and therefore, they were more at ease.

While implementation of the class facilitation

was varied and creative, almost every CFCT divided the class into discussion groups for the games and activities. All CFCTs came up with a digital presentation of some kind, usually a PowerPoint, Google Slides, or Prezi with video clips, still images from the films, and links to other audio and video related to the articles. Most teams also included a web-based game such as Kahoots, Jeopardy, or bingo. Discussion questions or key terms were presented using seek-n-finds, crossword puzzles, matching and ordering games. Some presented hand-outs to write on with the discussion questions for group activities.

As demonstrated by how students chose to facilitate, an important outcome of the class facilitation assignment is that students "revisit" an article. The CFCT presenting must read it multiple times in order to teach it. Their classmates will often have the article open during the facilitation in order to participate in the discussion and play the games. Not only are they engaged in the lesson but they will reference the article as part of that participation. This leads to in-depth discussions of not only the article content but the overall subject matter—which leads to deeper understanding and remembered knowledge. Students commented that after spending time learning to read articles, specifically figuring out how to break down articles into smaller chunks, they found it *easier to read textbooks* in their other classes. They also stated that *this was a lot more fun than if you'd just made us read a bunch of articles on our own.*

Conclusions

The initial idea for this assignment came, not as a plan to produce a pedagogical study, but simply an experiment to help students tackle a challenging skill. The concept was to combine the class facilitation assignment with library research education, rhetorical awareness, and writing practice in hopes that they would transfer the knowledge into future academic, professional, and personal pursuits. In the example for this essay, the chosen articles all examined social issues or human rights themes as a way to demonstrate how social action connects to academic research and writing—meeting the associated cultural diversity course goal—and how those things can come from popular culture.

Academic reading is associated with legitimation, thus students need to recognize that reading influential authors provides understanding of ideas at stake in the discourse community and entry into the discourse community (Hill and Meo 2015). Although it was sampled in two different writing courses, the collaborative class facilitation assignment can be adapted for any course and can be done using textbook chapters, creative texts, or websites. Teachers are able to bring students into the discourse community and control the course narrative through their choice of articles for the class facilitation assignment. Ultimately, an instructor's course goals determine the types of articles chosen, as long as they create the appropriate connecting narrative.

References

Collins, S. (2008). *The hunger games*. New York, NY: Scholastic Press.

Hermida, J. (2009). The importance of teaching academic reading skills in first-year university courses. *The International Journal of Research and Review, 3*, 20-30.

Hill, L., & Meo, A.I. (2015). A Bourdieusian approach to academic reading: reflections on a South African teaching experience. *Teaching in Higher Education, 20*(8), 845-856. Retrieved from http://dx.doi.org/10.1080/13562517.2015.1095178

Willfred, M. T. (2017). Collaborative Learning as a Discourse Strategy for Enhancing Academic Reading Skills Amongst First Year University Students. *Gender & Behavior, 15*(4), 10011-10037.

Resistive Pedagogy: Student-Facilitated Learning and Literacy through Zines

Jessica Vaught
Eastern Kentucky University

Zines are self-publications that contradict the process and content of mainstream media publication. In the classroom environment, zines are alternate, low-stakes opportunities within course assignments. They are characterized by their socio-political content, resisting the expectations of dominant cultural ideologies; therefore, zines earn the title of resistive texts. Visually, zines are characterized by their aesthetic of cutting, pasting, and copying handwritten texts and repurposed images alongside the language and grammar of the creator. This emphasis on creator-driven expression relates directly to the current discussion surrounding the inaccessibility of academic language, which suggests that some students are barred or discouraged from pursuing higher education as their level of both literacy and personal lingual skills are not acceptable or validated at the college level. By incorporating student production of zines as either workshops or instructional alternatives in place of traditional research or argumentative formal papers in introductory writing courses, teachers give students the opportunity to facilitate their own learning and enhance their literacy skills, as the nature of zines allows for the creators to use language and materials readily accessible to the creator.

Introduction

Zines are do-it-yourself (DIY) self-publications intended to contradict the process and content of mainstream media publications and are characterized by their socio-political content that resists dominant cultural ideologies, therefore dubbing zines "resistive texts" (Kempson, 2014) as accessibility and resistance are at the core of zines' production. This emphasis on creator-driven expression relates to the current discussion on the inaccessibility of academia, and more specifically academic language, which suggests that some students are barred or discouraged from pursuing higher education as their level of both literacy and personal lingual skills are not validated by college standards; oftentimes, students are encouraged to "code-switch" in their academic work, which entails knowing when and how to use non-standard versus academic language in the classroom (Epstein & Herring-Harris, 2011). This practice is problematic, however, as some scholars view code switching as potential linguistic prejudice that reinforces oppressive power structures which decide the languages with and without validity in academia (Dunstand & Jaeger, 2015). Zines encourage writers to communicate their content in ways comfortable and accessible to them.

Zines allow for students to see themselves in their writing and become more comfortable with writing as they generate more content; eventually, students will develop their own written voices and feel less intimidated by writing than before.

Introducing zines into the classroom setting has the potential to alleviate this discouragement; by incorporating student production of zines as either workshops or instructional alternatives or supplements to traditional formal papers in introductory writing courses. Instructors give students the opportunity to facilitate their own learning and improve their literacy skills through low-stakes writing assessments. Zines promote language and materials readily accessible to the creator and against dominant ideologies (in this case, academic language). On the topic of writing, Lindemann (1982) states in *A Rhetoric for Writing Teachers* that "most writing does not belong exclusively to any one category," and that the traditional academic implication that there is only one way to use proper language is linguistically inaccurate; which parallels the nature of zines.

Ultimately, the use of "resistive texts" (referred to as "resistive pedagogy" in this work) in the classroom aligns with both process and expressive pedagogy. Zines require students to develop their own writing processes that best suit their needs and styles as learners, which aligns with process pedagogy; zines also emphasize the importance of having a personal connection to the content itself, which aligns with expressive pedagogy. Zines, paralleled with process and expressive pedagogy, serve as an alternative medium to standard research papers and allow students to facilitate their own learning and increase their metacognitive and literacy skills by relieving the emphasis on academic language that may be inaccessible to students or bar them from academic achievement.

Strategy Overview
Zines

Zines are DIY self-publications. Originally, zines began in the format of either written or typed text alongside images that are cut and pasted onto variously sized booklets; once fully constructed, the booklets are then copied and mass produced. Zines have since modernized from their original format of the 1970s-1990s and can now be made either traditionally or by using more modern technology, such as designing the text and images on photo-shopping software to produce more professional-looking products. Zines can be individual publications, or exist as serial publications. Regardless, the focal point of creating zines is for the creator to choose a topic (or, in this case, a thesis) that is significant to him or her and then to communicate it through individually designed publications that do not adhere to traditional publication format.

Classroom Implication

Zines are ideal for student use due to their DIY nature. Students can utilize paper, scissors, glue and tape, writing implements, and digital programs such as Microsoft PhotoShop, Adobe InDesign, and Microsoft PowerPoint. Students construct zines individually or in small groups as an alternative assessment. Theoretically, an instructor could assign a prompt just as with traditional written work and, instead of creating a 4-5 page researched argument, students could create a 6-8 page researched argument in booklet format. All student learning outcomes would still apply toward the construction of the students' thesis and research, but the medium in which the content is presented would offer alternatives.

Pedagogical Alignment

Resistive pedagogy in the classroom incidentally aligns with expressive, process, and feminist pedagogy. The use of resistive pedagogy first and foremost correlates with expressive pedagogy, which draws on the importance of students writing on a topic in which they have great interest (Burnham & Powell, 2013). Expressive pedagogy intends for students to be more engaged with their work and develop their own voices. Alternative products such as zines potentially alleviate the pressure of conforming to academic language and allow for the gradual development of student voice.

In using resistive texts, instructors also draw upon process pedagogy. The goal of process pedagogy is to place more focus on the students' writing process instead of the students' final writing products, giving the students tools to use going forward in writing future works (Anson, 2013). Process pedagogy also stresses the importance of developing the structure of the overall work over mechanics such as syntax and grammar. Zines require that students think carefully, critically, and creatively about their process as they must choose how to represent their researched arguments in zine format, encouraging them to have pre-planning and brainstorming stages before putting their researched content together in a booklet. Students must have a "game plan" when brainstorming a topic, generating a thesis, completing research, and presenting content in a creative and thoughtful way, which ultimately develops a process. Zines also do not focus as much on dominant cultural and structural ideologies, under which academia falls; in zines, grammatical and syntax mechanics would not have precedence over the structure and flow of the zine itself as a unified work.

Resistive texts also align with feminist pedagogy. In feminist pedagogy, students use composition as a vehicle for self-discovery as they develop their own written voices and work with opposing ideas to construct a thesis based on their own beliefs (Micciche, 2013). As zines encourage the language of the creator, students get more practice in developing their voices and therefore discover themselves; likewise, the students use alternative mediums to mainstream publications to create a thesis-driven work that advocates for an idea of their own. Zines are an excellent way to incorporate feminist pedagogy not only for the students' opportunity for self-discovery and engagement with multiple sides to an issue, but also because they are introduced to accessibly, non-mainstream ideas, and advocating for their beliefs from their own standpoints in a civil, supported way.

Student-Centeredness

Self-Facilitated Learning through Metacognitive Strategies

Resistive texts are student-centered in nature as they require students to facilitate their own learning through the development and implementation of metacognitive strategies and therefore self-efficacy as learners. Three major metacognitive strategies employed by resistive texts are regulation of cognition, self-reflection, and critical and creative thinking.

When students begin working on their resistive texts, they must have a writing process for the work involved in constructing the content and constructing the zine as discussed in pedagogical alignment. Students need to set plans for themselves and regulate their own learning, setting goals for what needs to be completed first, outlining their product, and following the necessary steps until the final product's completion. Students also need to know the processes that best fit their learning and writing styles, with is also an act of metacognition as they reflect on themselves as learners and, more importantly in this case, as writers; these practices fall under the Metacognitive Awareness Inventory as regulation of cognition (VIU, 2018). Regulation of cognition also requires students to evaluate their progress and make changes as needed.

Evaluating on progress is, ultimately, self-reflection, which is another metacognitive act. When students evaluate their work and make decisions about effective strategies they are reflecting upon themselves as learners and developing writers. They reflect not only on what is and is not working, but also on the fact that their drafted work needs to be changed, which is a critical characteristic for students to have as writers. Having the ability to know oneself as a writer and revise with a positive growth mindset is crucial to students' overall academic success.

Finally, resistive texts in the classroom promote critical and creative thinking among students. When creating zines, students take their abilities to construct a written work to the next level. Students must have a process developed to present their work in a completely different medium that effectively communicates the key points of their work. Creative components lie in the students' ability to construct the zine itself.

Literacy and Voice

Resistive pedagogy is also student-centered in that it helps in both increasing students' written literacy and encouraging students' natural written voices. Writing brings out self-consciousness in students, which is further amplified when students have varying language proficiencies or dialects that deviate from Standard American English. Additionally, depending on student demographics, introductory college composition courses may be when students first work with writing, academic language, and rhetoric. This can lead to apprehensive, intimidated students having a lower likelihood of succeeding not only as writers, but in the field of academia. Incorporating zines into the classroom, increases the opportunity to exercise one's own voice and practice writing through low-stakes writing assessments, potentially facilitating student development in both literacy and voice.

When instructors implement resistive pedagogy in the classroom, they are assigning low-stakes writing assessments by assigning zines. Zines encourage the language that is accessible to the creator, which means the students can take a more familiar approach to writing their content. Low-stakes writing assignments are incredibly beneficial to the development of a writer as they allow students to communicate content and ideas in a comfortable language that is not jumbled by the students' attempts to sound academic. Both the Eberly Center of Carnegie Mellon University (2016) and scholar Peter Elbow (1997) note that students' written language reads as clumsy and awkward when they feel pressured to sound more academic and that low-stakes assignments give these students the opportunity to clearly express their ideas without the added obstacle of academic language.

Elbow (1997) also argues that, as students develop their writing voices and styles through low-stakes writing assessments, they ultimately perform better when the time comes to complete a high-risk writing assessment, such as a traditional, formal research paper. This results from students having opportunities to reflect on their writing, find the strategies that work best for them, and develop their voices without the added pressure and expectation to sound like a professional academic in an introductory course where the students are writing apprentices. Zines as low-risk assessments can ultimately contribute to students potentially increasing their literacy skills as they generate more content and exercise their writing processes leading up to higher-risk assessments.

Some students may even feel intellectually inferior not because of their dialect, but because of their lack of knowledge in the grammar mechanics of Standard American English. Students often dub themselves "bad writers" simply because their grammar skills are not of the highest caliber (Eberly, 2016). When students condemn themselves as "bad writers," especially when the reason being is that they do not feel comfortable with grammar mechanics, the students are barring themselves from achieving a positive growth mindset necessary to becoming a confident writer.

Zines encourage the creators to write in voices natural to themselves. This practice is extremely empowering to students as it allows them to see themselves in academic writing and therefore see themselves as academics. Many students write the way they speak, and some students know that their specific dialects and languages carry stigma in academic or professional settings. For example, a study of Appalachian students revealed that the students refrained from active participation in class for fear of seeming intellectually inferior due to their dialect (Dunstan & Jaeger, 2015). A separate study reported by *The New York Times* revealed that African American students also felt stigmatized by their dialects and believed themselves to be perceived as uneducated in the English language because of the way they spoke (Lee, 1994). When students harbor these stigmas about the way they write and speak, they cannot fully and confidently participate in writing as their authentic selves and achieve.

Regardless of the students' reason for feeling inadequate in the eyes of academia, all students should be able to see themselves represented in academic writing. Zines alleviate the pressure to code switch, which is a practice that only furthers the students' feelings that only one type of voice sounds professional enough to be in print. Students must feel empowered through education as well as validated in that their discourse community has value. In "When the First Voice You Hear is Not Your Own," Jacqueline Royster (1996) writes that all language communities should not only be taken seriously, but also critically inquired, stating "Those of us who love our own communities… who want to preserve consciously, critically, and also lovingly the record of good work within them must take high risk and give over the exclusivity of our rights to know." Academia needs to reflect its writers no matter the discourse community not only so that the writers can see themselves preserved, shared, and represented, but also so that the writers can reflect upon and discover themselves. Through writing zines, students see their language validated in an academic setting as the low-risk assessment asks that they communicate and reflect upon themselves as they are.

Final Thoughts

When instructors decide to implement resistive pedagogy in their classrooms, they offer their students the opportunity to become more comfortable and self-actualized as writers. Zines creative nature allows for students to become more engaged with their written work and provides students with more opportunities to generate more content, thus building their writing skills. If properly aligned with expressive process, and feminist pedagogy, resistive pedagogy has the potential to help improve the students' literacy skills and, arguably more importantly, help students develop their own written voices. Zines provide more seats at the table, allowing students to see themselves in a written work as valid voices important enough to be featured in academic work; for students to foster and implement positive growth mindsets, they must have this validation to move forward, hone their composition skills, and create the space they deserve.

References

Anson, C. (2013). Process pedagogy and its legacy. In G. Tate, A.T. Rupiper, H.B. Hessler, & K. Schick (Eds.), *A Guide to Composition Pedagogies*, New York, NY: Oxford UP.

Burnham, C., & Powell, R. (2013). Expressive pedagogy: Practice/theory, theory/practice. In G. Tate, A.T. Rupiper, H.B. Hessler, & K. Schick (Eds.), *A Guide to Composition Pedagogies*, New York, NY: Oxford UP.

Dunstan, S., B., & Jaeger, A., J. (2015). Dialect an influence on the academic experiences of college students. *The Journal of Higher Education, 86*(5), 777-803. DOI: 10.1353/jhe.2015.0026

Eberly Center of Carnegie Mellon University. (2016). Students may be intimidated by writing and lack of confidence in their abilities. *Carnegie Mellon University*, Retrieved from https://www.cmu.edu/teaching/solveproblem/strat-cantwrite/cantwrite-05.html

Elbow, P. (1997). High stakes and low stakes in assigning and responding to writing. *New Directions for Teaching & Learning, 69*, 5-13.

Epstein, P., & Herring-Harris, L. (2011). Honors dialect and increasing student performance in standard English. *National Writing Project.* Retrieved from https://www.nwp.org/cs/public/print/resource/3655

Kempson, M. (2014). My version of feminism: Subjectivity, DIY and the feminist zine. *Social Movement Studies, 4*(4). doi.org/10.1080/14742837.2014.945157

Lee, F. (1994). Lingering conflict in the schools: Black dialect vs. standard speech. *The New York Times,* Retrieved from https://www.nytimes.com/1994/01/05/nyregion/lingering-conflict-in-the-schools-black-dialect-vs-standard-speech.html

Lindemann, E. (1982). *A rhetoric for writing teachers* (4th ed.). New York, NY: Oxford UP.

Micciche, L. R. (2013). Feminist pedagogies. In G. Tate, A.T. Rupiper, H.B. Hessler, & K. Schick (Eds.), *A Guide to Composition Pedagogies*, New York, NY: Oxford UP.

Royster, J. (1996). When the first voice you hear is not your own. *College Composition and Communication, 47*(1). Retrieved from https://www.jstor.org/stable/358272?seq=1#page_scan_tab_contents

VIU. (2018). Ten metacognitive teaching strategies. *Center for Innovation and Excellence in Learning.* Retrieved from https://ciel.viu.ca/teaching-learning-pedagogy/designing-your-course/how-learning-works/ten-metacognitive-teaching-strategies

Using Assessment Data to Create Targeted Instructor Training

John Strada, Krista M. Kimmel, & Jennifer L. Fairchild
Eastern Kentucky University

As part of a university-mandated, biennial general education assessment, a southern regional university's Department of Communication collected data (n=57) from basic course speech assignments during the 2016-2017 academic year. A team of faculty members analyzed the results of the assessment, and from those results developed specific training recommendations for all communication basic course instructors. The basic course co-directors then created and implemented a targeted instructor training program for basic course faculty. The implications of such training programs for general education faculty, particularly adjunct faculty, are discussed.

Introduction

American institutions of higher education are held accountable to a number of entities: their governing boards; state and federal government; accrediting agencies; and the general public (Schmidtlein & Berdahl, 2011). Accrediting agencies, which include regional, faith-based, private career, and programmatic accreditors, ensure the quality of postsecondary institutions. Regional accrediting agencies require colleges and universities to provide evidence of institutional effectiveness and progress on student learning outcomes on a periodic basis, usually every five to 10 years. Further, regional accreditation holds substantial financial implications for postsecondary institutions, as federal financial aid is accessible only to students attending a regionally-accredited institution (Cragg, Henderson, Fitzgerald, & Griffith, 2013). Given that nearly 60% of all undergraduate students receive federal financial aid (NCES, 2013), regional accreditation is of significant consequence.

In addition, postsecondary institutions are now tasked with providing data that demonstrate their effectiveness on defined outcomes (Schmidtlein & Berdahl, 2011). One of the ways that this directive can be accomplished is though the collection of course assessment data. Assessment is the process of "declaring goals, defining criteria for success, providing evidence to illustrate the success of goals, and indicating changes to be implemented as a result" (Cragg et al., 2013, p. 90). In short, assessment holds departments and programs accountable for their teaching and students' learning.

Assessment is often viewed by faculty as a burdensome, intrusive task mandated by interfering forces. However, the purpose of collecting assessment data should extend further than a means simply to document students' progress on learning outcomes or fulfill an administrative mandate. Ideally, assessment is intended to create meaningful change and encourage continuous improvement (Cragg et al., 2013). Additionally, assessment should encourage faculty members to work together to create and reinforce learning goals (Wagenaar, 2011).

One specific way to accomplish this meaningful change is to use assessment data to create targeted instructor training, with the goal of encouraging intentional and informed teaching of general education courses. Several studies have demonstrated the importance for professional development opportunities and support services for adjunct faculty (Gadberry & Burnstad, 2005; Hoyt, 2012; Meixner, Kruck, & Madden, 2010; Milliken & Jurgens, 2008). However, as Milliken and Jurgens (2008) contend, adjunct faculty often are unaware of training and professional development opportunities that are available to full-time faculty. But as Hoyt (2012) asserts, adjunct faculty seek such opportunities, and Milliken and Jurgens found annual orientations/meetings for adjunct faculty were particularly valued.

With this is mind, the co-directors of the general education communication courses ("basic course") at a southern, regional university devised and implemented a training program for all faculty teaching the general education communication courses. The training's content was derived from insights that emerged from the analysis of assessment data collected during the 2016-2017 academic year. The training initiative was designed to strengthen the instructors' awareness and understanding of student learning outcomes, assessment rubrics, and the implications of the assessment data. In essence, the training's objective was to increase the instructors' interest and engagement in the assessment process. Upon completion of the training, the instructors would then be able to execute specific pedagogical strategies addressing the weaknesses revealed in the assessment results. After the next assessment cycle, the data would reflect any improvement on student learning outcomes. While this article focuses specifically on demonstrating a training developed for use in basic communication courses, the general process of converting assessment data to training content should be generalizable to other courses and disciplines.

The Assessment Process

Every other year, the authors' institution requires assessment of student progress toward general education learning goals. Two communication studies (CMS) courses, CMS 100: Introduction to Human Communication, and CMS 210: Public Speaking, fulfill requirements of the university's general education curriculum. During the most recent assessment cycle, 30 sections of CMS 100 and eight sections of CMS 210 were offered in the Fall 2016 semester. The final speech assignment from each course was selected as the source of data that would be used to assess student progress on learning courtcomes. Each speech was recorded and the video was uploaded into a secure, online archive. This university's general education assessment guidelines ask for a random sample of 5% of student work for each class. Since the requisite university class size for general education courses is 25, two speeches from each section were chosen to compose the data sample. An online random number generator was used to determine the roster numbers for the students selected. Three faculty members were chosen to assess the sampled speeches. These faculty members reviewed several speeches together to assure general inter-rater reliability, and then evenly divided the speeches among themselves for the assessment. The assessment was performed using the University's *General Education Oral Communication Rubric*. This rubric was developed using the guidelines outlined in the National Communication Association's (2007) *Competent Speaker Speech Evaluation Form*. The university form consists of seven categories: structure; content; context; audience awareness; oral delivery; nonverbal delivery; and presentation aids. Each category is rated on a four-point ordinal scale, with 4= accomplished; 3= competent; 2= developing; and 1= beginning.

Results of Data Collection

The following raw results were compiled using frequency data from the evaluators' assessment ratings of speeches in CMS 100 (n=41) and CMS 210 (n=16) courses. In order to be determined "competent" in a category, the speaker had to earn a rating of three or four. The communication department's assessment goal is that 70% of all students in the basic course should emerge the course as "competent."

CMS 100		CMS 210	
Category % Competent		Category % Competent	
Structure	41.66%	Structure	50%
Content	24.39%	Content	31%
Context	39.02%	Context	63%
Audience	29.27%	Audience	56%
Oral Deliv.	58.54%	Oral Deliv.	69%
Nonverbal	14.63%	Nonverbal	25%
Pres Aids	19.51%	Pres Aids	13%

Initial analysis of the data from both classes showed relative strengths in oral delivery and speech structure, mixed results in context and audience analysis, and generally poor performance in nonverbal delivery, speech content, and presentation aid usage. However, the basic course co-directors recognized the limitations of relying simply on the assessment's raw results to initiate meaningful changes to the courses. Subsequently, each category was further analyzed to determine possible causes for the scores, and to devise specific strategies that could be used to improve performance in each category. As suggested by Wagenaar (2011), this further analysis would enable faculty members to define course and assignment goals more clearly.

Enhanced Analysis of the Seven Rubric Categories

Structure: The review of the sample speeches in both CMS 100 and CMS 210 indicated that deficiencies in this category were due predominantly to students using introductions and conclusions that did not contain the required structural elements, or having no formal introduction or conclusion at all. From this analysis, the assessment team recommended that the basic co-directors review the required elements for speech introductions and conclusions with the CMS 210 instructors. Additionally, the team suggested that instructors emphasize to their students the reasoning for and importance of including all required elements of speech introductions and conclusions in their presentations.

Content: The overall score for speech content was extremely low across all courses. These scores were found to be primarily influenced by students who either cited sources incorrectly, or failed to cite any sources whatsoever. To address this deficiency, the assessment team recommended that instructors review proper in-speech citation protocol with their students. Additionally, instructors were asked to review the importance of citing sources to avoid accusations of academic dishonesty.

Context: While the context score was the second highest assessment category for the CMS 210 courses, it was as weakness in the CMS 100 course. These results were produced by the students delivering the "wrong kind of speech." In this specific case, CMS 210 students were assigned a persuasive speech, but delivered an informative presentation, and CMS 100 students were assigned an informative speech, but delivered a persuasive presentation. The assessment team could not determine if the disconnect was due to student error, or because of the instructor failing to assign the correct type of speech to his/her students. The team also noted that due to the survey nature the CMS 100 course, instructors spent considerably less time providing instruction about speech construction and delivery. This difference in instruction could explain the discrepancy in scores between the CMS 100 and the CMS 210 course. To improve context scores, the assessment team recommended that the basic course co-directors review the course assignment expectations with the course instructors. The team also recommended that the instructors clearly articulate the expectations for each speech assignment to their students.

Audience Awareness: The assessment team noted the speakers' topics were either not appropriate for the occasion or were not tailored to their specific audience. Additionally, the speakers generally lacked awareness of/connection to their audiences. To improve the audience awareness scores, the assessment team recommended that instructors stress the importance of audience analysis and audience-centered speaking with their students.

Oral Delivery: Oral delivery was the strongest category in the entire assessment. The assessment team conjectured that these scores were generally high because our students received extensive writing instruction in high school, and those skills emerged in students' speech development and delivery. The team recommended that instructors continue to emphasize to students the importance of effective and appropriate language while delivering their speeches. The instructors were also asked to continue to encourage creative, original speech topics and delivery.

Nonverbal Delivery: The nonverbal delivery scores were extremely low in both courses. These low scores were initially surprising to the assessment team, as a significant portion of course instruction time in both courses was devoted to nonverbal delivery. The assessment team noted that students were particularly deficient in the areas of eye contact; voice variety; purposeful movement; and delivery energy/enthusiasm. Additionally, many students delivered manuscript speeches instead of the extemporaneous delivery prescribed in the course. To remedy this, the assessment team recommended that the basic course co-directors review the standards for nonverbal delivery behaviors in the basic courses with the course instructors. Instructors were also asked to utilize more instructional time to teaching extemporaneous delivery skills, and to reinforce the expectation that speech assignments will be delivered using an extemporaneous style.

Presentation Aids: The assessment results from presentation aid usage was poor in both of the courses. The assessment team found that students who were deficient in this category either did not follow proper usage rules for presentation aids, or did not use presentation aids at all. However, the assessment team noted two mitigating factors that may have influenced this low assessment score. First, in many cases the presentation aids could not be viewed at all in the video recording of the speech, making it impossible to determine if the student had a presentation aid, or if they had used the presentation aid properly. In these cases, the presentation aid score had to be marked as a "1." Additionally, the team learned from informal student feedback that several course instructors may not have followed the basic course directive requiring presentation aids for all final speeches. The assessment team recommended that the basic course directors review the expectations for presentation aid use with the CMS 210 instructors to ensure that all instructors assigned the required presentation aid usage in CMS 210 speeches. Furthermore, CMS 210 instructors were asked to make sure the presentation aids were visible in frame during the recording of the speech presentations.

Implementation

The targeted instructor training developed from enhanced analysis of the assessment data was included as part of the annual beginning of the academic year basic course faculty meeting. The majority of the meeting's agenda was devoted to a discussion of the results of the assessment data. All basic course instructors were provided with a copy of the oral communication rubric and the raw assessment results (i.e. frequency scores for each of the categories on the rubric; percentages of students achieving a score of "competent" in each category). The basic course co-directors shared their perspective from the enhanced data analysis, and then asked the instructors for their own additional interpretations of each category on the rubric. Finally, the instructors collectively viewed sample speeches from the data set and practiced rating those speeches according the rubric.

These activities resulted in an engaging, fruitful discussion. First, instructors appeared somewhat surprised by the overall poor results on student learning outcomes reflected in the assessment data. Many instructors simply did not realize the weaknesses the students demonstrated across multiple categories in the rubric. Second, the instructors benefited from a detailed explanation of the rubric used in assessment. For example, many faculty members did not realize that the assessment team must assign the lowest score of "1" for presentation aid use if the aid is not visible in the recorded video. They also recognized that students' deficiency in citing sources yielded poor results in the category of content. Third, the exercise of scoring sample speeches as a group allowed the instructors to discuss what speaking behaviors are deemed "beginning," "developing," "competent," and "accomplished." For instance, if a student lacks eye contact with the audience, but displays strong nonverbal delivery skills otherwise, should that student receive a score of "developing" or "competent"? Finally, the instructors were eager to share with one another best practices for teaching public speaking. The faculty members offered instructional strategies related to each category on the rubric, with many instructors stating they planned to implement these practices into their teaching the upcoming year.

Implications

Assessment is an important part of the landscape of contemporary higher education. Dwindling state appropriations, competition for philanthropic support, and transitions toward performance-based funding are driving the current conversation of assessment and accountability (McGuinness, 2011). In addition, regional accreditors are demanding more accountability from academic departments than a mere token plan for improvement. Rather, they are seeking specific examples of implemented change, and subsequently, documented improvement in student learning outcomes (Morest, 2009). The use of targeted instructor trainings, based on assessment results, are a tangible means of demonstrating to both administrators and accrediting bodies that the collected data are being used to create meaningful change in courses and programs. Moreover, departments will be able to hone their long-term goals and expectations based on those tangible data. Finally, collection of assessment data over time can provide basic course directors with concrete evidence that the implemented changes have produced the desired outcomes and improvements in student learning. If no improvements are found, faculty members will be better able to target their efforts to identify the root causes of these deficiencies. Future training and development programs may be needed to produce the desired student outcomes.

In summary, academic departments can proactively create an assessment, analysis, and implementation process similar to the one described in this article for their own advantage. By utilizing assessment data more purposefully, departments and programs will be better equipped to manage the challenges ahead, and most importantly, accurately measure the success of their students.

References

Cragg, K.M., Henderson, A.E., Fitzgerald, B.D., & Griffith, R.A. (2013). Administrative aspects of accreditation and assessment. In P.J. Schloss & K.M. Cragg (Eds.), *Organization and administration in higher education* (pp. 80-100). New York: Routledge.

EKU General Education Oral Communication Rubric. (2009). Retrieved from http://gened.eku.edu/sites/gened.eku.edu/files/files/GE_Rubric_1C.pdf

Gadberry, J., & Burnstad, H. (2005). Integrating adjuncts into the community through professional development support. *Academic Leader, 21*(7), 1-6.

Hoyt, J. J. (2012). Predicting the satisfaction and loyalty of adjunct faculty. *Journal of Continuing Higher Education, 60*(3), 132-142.

Meixner, C., Kruck, S. E., & Madden, L. T. (2010). Inclusion of part-time faculty for the benefit of faculty and students. *College Teaching, 58*(4), 141-147.

Milliken, T. F., & Jurgens, J. C. (2008). Assessing the needs of human services adjunct faculty: Uncovering strategies for retaining quality instructors. *Human Service Education, 28*(1), 29-43.

McGuinness, A.C. (2011). The states and higher education. In P.G. Altbach, P.J. Gumport, & R.O. Berdahl (Eds.), *American higher education in the twenty-first century: Social, political and economic challenges* (pp. 139-169). Baltimore: The Johns Hopkins University Press.

Morest, V. S. (2009). Accountability, accreditation, and continuous improvement: Building a culture of evidence. *New Directions for Institutional Research, (143)*, 17- 27.

National Center for Education Statistics. (2013). 2011-2012 National Postseconday Student Aid Study (NPSAS: 12): Student Financial Aid Estimates from 2011-12. Retrieved from https://nces.ed.gov/pubs2013/2013165.pdf

National Communication Association (2007). The competent speaker speech evaluation form (2nd ed.). Retrieved from https://ams.natcom.org/uploadedFiles/Teaching_and_Learning/Assessment_Resources/PDF-Competent_Speaker_Speech_Evaluation_Form_2ndEd.pdf

Schmidtlein, F.A., & Berdahl, R.O. (2011). Autonomy and accountability: Who controls academe? In P.G. Altbach, P.J. Gumport, & R. O. Berdahl (Eds.), *American higher education in the twenty-first century: Social, political, and economic challenges* (pp. 69-87). Baltimore: The Johns Hopkins University Press.

Wagenaar, T. (2011). Why do I like assessment? Let me count the ways. *Chronicle of Higher Education, 57*(26), 35.

www.ingramcontent.com/pod-product-compliance
Lightning Source LLC
Chambersburg PA
CBHW080550170426
43195CB00016B/2746